Powerful
Questions and
Techniques
For
Coaches and
Therapists

By

Tim Hallbom

Nick LeForce

Kris Hallbom

Published by:

Inner Works Press

© 2019

Tim Hallbom, Nick LeForce,

and Kris Hallbom

For inquiries:

nlnlp@me.com

Acknowledgements

The authors would like to acknowledge the following people who have helped make this work possible by their contributions to the field of NLP and to the practice of coaching.

Richard Bandler and John Grinder for their brilliant developments in creating the field of NLP and their models, Virginia Satir, Milton Erickson and Fritz Perls; Robert Dilts, our colleague and teacher who has made so many of the ongoing developments in the fields of NLP and Coaching; Steve and Connirae Andreas for their contributions in making NLP more robust and accessible; Rodger Bailey and Leslie Cameron Bandler for their work with Meta Programs and criteria; Jan Elfline for her pioneering efforts in bringing NLP into the world of coaching; Ian McDermott for his trailblazing work with NLP and Coaching as well as his several fine books on the subject and, finally, Thomas Leonard and Tim Gallwey for helping to create the field of coaching in the first place.

The authors also want to acknowledge coaches Karna Sundby, Epiphany Shaw, Dan Ross, Holly Stokes and Austin Shaw for their contributions to the case examples included in the appendix!

Powerful Questions and Techniques for Coaches and Therapists

Contents

Introduction

Our mission is to discover *what works* in the realms of human effectiveness, change, interpersonal communications, and in coaching and psychotherapy and to share it with others. Furthermore, we want to provide information and skill development with the highest possible quality, integrity, and with a deep commitment to the personal and professional development of each person with whom we work.

The goal of this book is to offer clear and specific how to's to increase your effectiveness as a coach or therapist. Of course, the work you do needs to be done with your heart and spirit, and with your own unique blend of skills and resources. When you read this book and put the practices into action, you will improve your game as a coach or therapist. We have tested and shared these methods with participants in our coach trainings across the globe and we are happy to share them with you in book form.

We hope you are so inspired by each chapter that you want to read more and that you will, in your own way, read the book "cover to cover," bookmarking parts and passages that serve you, and use the book as a guide and reference in the future!

This book was rewritten and adapted from our earlier book, *Coaching in the Workplace*, which was written to give managers useful coaching skills. Over the years, we received lots of feedback from many professional coaches and therapists *outside of the workplace* who found the first book so useful. This second edition is addressed to all who provide some variation of life coaching.

WHO WE ARE:

NICK LEFORCE:

Nick LeForce, also known as the Transformational Poet, has over 35 years of experience in the field of human communication and development. He's also an internationally recognized trainer in the fields of Neuro Linguistic Programming (NLP) and coaching; and has authored several books on NLP, coaching, hypnosis and poetry.

Since 1982, Nick has studied extensively with leaders in the field of NLP. He is a certified Practitioner, Master Practitioner, and Trainer in NLP as well as Ericksonian Hypnotherapy. He has designed and delivered certified NLP and Coaching programs throughout Asia, Europe, Mexico, Australia and the USA. He is particularly known for his language skills and elegant use of poetry to help people find their own voice, reclaim their soul, and walk a path with heart.

Nick is the president of Inner Works, established in 1992, a coaching and training company located in Northern California, providing executive coaching services to businesses as well as personal coaching services to individuals.

In addition to being a professional coach, Nick has served as a core trainer for the International Coaching Federation (ICF) Approved Coach Training program offered through NLP Institute of California and the Academy of Leadership Coaching and NLP since 2002. He holds a Masters degree in Rehabilitation Administration and undergraduate degrees in Psychology and Social Welfare. You can visit his website at: www.nickleforce.com

TIM HALLBOM:

Tim Hallbom is an internationally known trainer and developer in the fields of coaching, hypnotherapy and Neuro Linguistic Programming. He is the co-author of the books *Beliefs: Pathways to Health and Well-Being*, *NLP: The New Technology of Achievement*, and *Innovations in NLP*.

He has been involved in the field of NLP since 1979 and has been delivering trainings throughout the world since then. Tim has always been more than a trainer. Throughout his career he has consistently provided therapy, coaching and consulting with individuals and organizations around the globe.

Tim has also contributed significantly to the body of knowledge in the fields of coaching, human behavior and change. He has refined and championed such processes as reimprinting, working with allergies, integrating conflicting beliefs, and using eye-accessing cues for discovery and change. He has developed a number of popular NLP change techniques, including ones for changing limiting beliefs, working with double binds, using eye cues for discovering the origins of any issue, working with health-related issues and business communications. He co-developed the initial protocol along with Steve Andreas for the trauma process, Reconsolidation of Traumatic Memories (RTM) – which has been scientifically shown to be effective in treating PTSD. You can visit his website at: www.timhallbom.com

KRIS HALLBOM:

Kris Hallbom is an internationally recognized NLP trainer, coach and author. She is the co-founder of the NLP Coaching Institute and has been actively involved in the field of NLP since 1988. She is also the co-developer of the WealthyMind™ Program, which has been taught to live audiences in over 20 countries and has helped thousands of people create more of what they want in their lives.

Recognized for her ability to translate complex ideas into practical skills, and for her warm, approachable style, Kris has trained and coached clients throughout Europe, Australia, Japan, Mexico, Canada and the USA. She is a contributing author to the best-selling books, *Alternative Medicine: The Definitive Guide* and *Innovations in NLP*. She has also produced numerous video and audio downloads on wealth consciousness, NLP coaching, and systems thinking.

Kris began studying Neuro-Linguistic Programming in 1987 while obtaining her university degree in Psychology and went on to become a master practitioner and certified trainer of NLP. She became a professional coach in 1996 and has done over five thousand hours of professional coaching with her clients and students. She does most of her coaching on the telephone and through Zoom, and has an international array of clients. You can visit her website at: www.krishallbom.com.

How This Book Is Organized

This book is divided into five sections as follows:

Section 1: Overview provides a general overview of coaching, how coaching differs from other approaches, and who provides coaching to employees in an organization.

Section 2: Coaching Process gives an understanding of the coaching process from beginning to end, including some assessment processes (Universal Cycles of Change and Meta-Programs).

Section 3: Coaching 101 The basics here offer useful communication skills and interactive skills for all phases of the coaching process.

Section 4: Managing Client Sessions gives a model for managing coaching sessions and specific steps or processes useful in all client sessions, such as gaining rapport, setting outcomes, and managing states.

Section 5: Techniques addresses a variety of specific interventions for specific situations.

Overview

WHY COACHING?

There is a unique, energy-driven relationship between two individuals unlike any other which is discovered and developed through the process of coaching. Coaching goes well-beyond collegial support or mentorship between family, friends, or business associates and has become a viable and popular career opportunity. Coaching is the ideal profession for those who have talent and interest in directing and motivating the success of others. An effective coaching career is highly rewarding because the coach can witness monumental improvements in the lives of their clients The rippling impact their clients have in the world around them makes coaching one of the most influential and fulfilling professions to pursue.

Those who hire a coach know that working with someone who can assist them to reach greater levels of success provides an edge that cannot be found in any other way. Videos and books will never produce the results that a coach can help you bring into reality because a coach is focused on your goals, assessing your strengths and weaknesses while communicating one on one to you about your life and your needs. Essentially, coaching transports the person from where they are to where they want to be through the interpersonal association of a coach and client.

Just as seasoned athletes hire a personal coach to push them beyond their current limits, to inspire them and keep them on track, a person hires a coach to help define and achieve desired goals and to perfect desired skills and abilities. There can be as many coach-types as there are areas of interest. For example, someone can be a marketing coach, a writing coach, a public speaking coach, a business coach, etc.

This book will give you the coaching tools you need to take your clients to the next level and become a stand-out professional in your chosen coaching field. The skills learned in this book will allow you to grow both your business and income as a premiere coaching expert. It will provide you with an understanding of the coaching relationship and how to use the most effective skills in whatever field of coaching or therapy you work within. It will help you and your client to set higher goals, make better decisions, take action to accomplish goals, and utilize natural strengths.

When properly used coaching can:

- Create stronger interpersonal relationships
- Empower the client
- Identify client strengths
- Identify client values
- Set challenging and realistic goals
- Improve decision-making skills
- Improve problem-solving skills
- Heighten commitment to tasks and assignments
- Provide effective accountability
- Tap into motivation
- Release creativity
- Increase morale
- Provide direction for client development

WHAT IS COACHING?

Coaching, as defined by the International Coach Federation, is "an ongoing partnership that helps clients produce fulfilling results in their personal and professional lives. Through the process of coaching, clients deepen their learning, improve their performance, and enhance their quality of life."

"Coaching is an interactive process that helps individuals and organizations to develop more rapidly and produce more satisfying results. As a result of coaching, clients set better goals, take more action, make better decisions, and more fully use their natural strengths."

"Coaches are trained to listen and observe, to customize their approach to the individual client's needs, and to elicit solutions and strategies from the client. They believe that the coach's job is to provide support to enhance the skills, resources, and creativity that the client already has. While the coach provides an objective perspective, the client is responsible for taking the steps to produce the results he or she desires."

The ICF goes on to describe the coaching sessions as follows: "In each meeting, the client chooses the focus of conversation while the coach listens and contributes observations and questions. This interaction creates clarity and moves the client into action. Coaching accelerates the client's progress by providing greater focus and awareness of choice. Coaching concentrates on where clients are today and what they are willing to do to get where they want to be tomorrow."

WHAT IS THE FOCUS OF COACHING?

Master Certified Coach Jan Elfline describes the coaching profession by saying, "Like counseling, it is client centered and individual. Like consulting, it is outcome oriented, dealing in visions and actions. The major difference between masterful training, therapy, consulting, or mentoring and masterful coaching can be described quite simply: the coach does not have the answers; the coach does not provide expertise; a coach operates from the presupposition that clients have all the resources they need, including the ability to discover and utilize resources."

Coaching allows clients to work and think more consciously and deliberately. It increases awareness of the choices the client makes and how those choices contribute to the quality of his or her life. The coach provides support for the client to develop capabilities, widen behavioral flexibility, try the unfamiliar, and venture into new territory. Through taking action, clients become aware, at a deep level, of their ability to make choices, take action, and to create their lives. The credit goes to the client, not the coach.

The late Thomas Leonard, one of the pioneers in the field of coaching, suggested that the purpose of coaching is to set more effective, achievable goals, accomplish more than you would have without coaching and to stay focused to achieve better results more quickly.

COACHING SKILLS AND PSYCHOTHERAPY

If you are a therapist, please know that all of the coach tools, skills and techniques can be used in a psychotherapeutic practice to enhance your work and help clients achieve successful outcomes. The work is testable, so at the end of a session, you can mark the client's progress.

NEURO-LINGUISTIC PROGRAMMING OR NLP

Many of the techniques and processes described in this book are derived from Neuro-Linguistic Programming (NLP). NLP started as a solution-oriented model of effectiveness and was originally used mainly as a cognitive-behavioral psychology. In this sense, it has always been closely affiliated with coaching. Since NLP studies the structure of experience, it can be applied in any human activity, and has been used successfully in counseling psychology, education, business, law, and many other fields. The initial developers in the field of NLP were John Grinder and Richard Bandler at the University of California at Santa Cruz in the Mid 1970s. Since then, many people have contributed to the field. For more information, the book *NLP: The New Technology of Achievement* is a good place to begin.

NLP and coaching are a perfect marriage because NLP offers a powerful framework for understanding people and a set of specific techniques useful in coaching. NLP is a field of study and can be applied in many ways while coaching is a vehicle to help a person move from the present to a desired future. NLP provides specific "how to" skills to create change in one's self and assist others in becoming more resourceful and effective. The table below summarizes the relationship between NLP and coaching.

NLP is:	Coaching is:
<ul><li>A field of study</li><li>A behavioral technology</li><li>A collection of change techniques</li><li>A methodology</li><li>A skill set</li></ul>	<ul><li>A vehicle, and an application of NLP and other communication models.</li><li>A method of getting from one place to another</li><li>A skill set</li></ul>

THE COACH-CLIENT RELATIONSHIP

Throughout the book, we will refer to the person being coached as "the client. It is critical to define the coaching relationship so that the client understands the roles their coach will fulfill, as well as their own responsibilities in the *coach-client relationship*. The main difference between coaching and other approaches is that the coach does not provide the answers. The entire goal of coaching is to bring out what is within the client, tapping into the client's own inner wisdom, strength, and talent, and working to bring out the best in the person. The specifics of the coaching relationship are defined through the coach contract, which will be discussed in detail within the next section, *Section Two: The Coaching Process.*

The Coaching Process

Coaching is a complex process. A coach must understand the steps of the process in order to guide the client effectively and accomplish the necessary steps in the coaching process. The *Coaching Relationship Mind Map* and the *Coach Session Overview* found in this book give the coach the tools to negotiate the process from start to end.

The *Coaching Relationship Mind Map* serves the coach by providing a map to negotiate the entire process of coaching. The coach uses the map to understand the major steps of the coaching process, to accomplish each step successfully, and to keep track of what to do next in the process. The coach can keep the larger picture in mind while attending to the specific needs of the client at each step along the way.

Most of the time is spent in the circle labeled "coaching sessions." The *Coach Session Overview*, found at the beginning of Section 4 on *Managing Client Sessions* is a separate mind map offering an overview of the process of conducting a coaching session. You can use these two maps as a coach to navigate the entire coaching relationship effectively and successfully.

THE COACH CONTRACT

The relationship between the coach and the client is consciously crafted through a defined relationship agreement or coaching contract. In the field of coaching, this contract is often referred to as a "Designed Alliance" because it is a formal, contracted relationship that is updated through time in the coaching relationship. This contract defines the roles of the parties and how the coach will serve the client and assist the client to achieve agreed desired results. The primary role of the coach is to ask high quality, powerful questions that stimulate the client to set their own goals, find their own motivation, keep on track, and revise or assess goals as challenges come up along the way. The primary role of the client is to be open and committed to the coaching process as a means of personal and professional development.

THE COACHING RELATIONSHIP

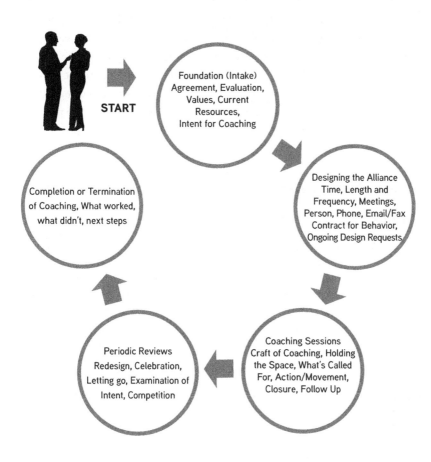

START

Foundation (Intake)
Agreement, Evaluation,
Values, Current
Resources,
Intent for Coaching

Designing the Alliance
Time, Length and
Frequency, Meetings,
Person, Phone, Email/Fax
Contract for Behavior,
Ongoing Design Requests

Completion or Termination
of Coaching, What worked,
what didn't, next steps

Coaching Sessions
Craft of Coaching, Holding
the Space, What's Called
For, Action/Movement,
Closure, Follow Up

Periodic Reviews
Redesign, Celebration,
Letting go, Examination of
Intent, Competition

Some aspects of the coaching contract (the frequency and duration of calls or meetings, the context—whether in person or on the telephone) are set out at the beginning of the coaching relationship and probably won't change. But it is important to note that the coach/client interaction is dynamic: it is fluid and adapts as the client grows and evolves. Agreements about the primary focus of the coaching content, the kinds of questions and interventions used by the coach, the degree of accountability, and how the coach can best serve the client may change over time. What has worked in the past might not work in the current situation. The coach and client, together, evaluate and adjust what they are doing and how it is affecting the progress of the client. The coaching contract is called a "designed alliance" because periodic adjustments to the contracted relationship are consciously discussed to make the coaching more powerful. Successful coaching is truly a collaborative process and the client contributes as much as the coach. The coach contract is a process of working out these relationship dynamics in a conscious manner.

Suggested Coaching Questions for Creating the Contract:

Initially-

- What do you want in (or from) a coach?
- How do you want to use me as your coach?
- Tell me what you know about how you get motivated to take action.
- What help do you need to move more quickly toward your goals?
- Do you want me to hold you accountable to take action?
- Do you want in–between assignments?

Ongoing -

- What is working?
- What might we want to change?

COACHING CYCLES

Unlike therapy or some forms of consulting, the coaching agreement typically specifies time parameters for the coaching relationship. These parameters, or coaching cycles, require the coach and client to review the coaching relationship and adjust or discontinue the relationship depending on results and client needs. Coaching cycles are typically defined by number of sessions. For instance, a common coaching cycle is six sessions, which is sufficient to allow the coach and client to develop a powerful coaching relationship but short enough to keep coaching focused and on track. A coaching cycle may be organized around a time frame (e.g. 3- or 6-months), especially if the client is using coaching to help with a specific project or time-framed issue. The coaching cycle is agreed up front and the client commits the designated cycle.

At the end of the cycle, the coach and client hold a review session and decide to contract for another round, alter the agreement, or to close the coaching process.

This session allows both parties to:

- Assess the client's progress towards agreed goals
- Review accomplishments
- Backtrack or review highlights of the coaching process
- Revisit the client's values and, if appropriate, life as a whole to put coaching into perspective
- Determine whether or not to continue for another cycle of coaching

If continuing:

- Re-contract for additional sessions
- Monitor and adjust the coaching relationship
- Identify what has worked and what might need adjusting in the coaching process
- Determine whether or not to change the primary focus

If closing:

- Get feedback from client about yourself as a coach
- Determine the next steps for the client
- If the coach is independent of the company: Get a testimonial from client (if willing and it is appropriate) and ask for referrals from client.

INTAKE

The intake or foundation meeting is your opportunity to discover what is important to the client and how you can serve her as a coach. The value of taking time with the intake meeting cannot be overstated. This meeting allows you to define your role as a coach and to co-create the coaching relationship. As a professional, you should be clear about the ground rules in the coaching relationship, what you expect from the client, and what the client can count on from you. Discuss confidentiality and the ethics and standards that guide your behavior.

Coaching is not a packaged service or product but a relationship that is unique to each client. The two of you will tailor an alliance that is intended to serve the client. This means that you encourage him/her to express needs and concerns, to make requests of you as a coach, and to ask for changes in the ongoing coaching relationship.

The intake meeting differs from later coaching in that you (the coach) will be setting the agenda for the appointment. To structure the intake session, decide what information you want from the client and how to use the time. Determine the time frame you need to establish the coaching relationship, set agreements, and get the intake information you decide you need to work effectively with the client. Typical intake appointments are one and a half to two hours. Whatever you decide for your overall time frame, it is important to allot time to each part: getting rapport and gathering basic information about the client, determining the focus of coaching, designing the alliance with the client, and agreeing on logistics. You may have written work that you ask the client to do before or during the intake appointment. So be sure you have enough time to cover everything and set the stage for a powerful coaching relationship. Remember that this is a map, a plan, and that few, if any appointments, will follow the plan exactly.

Schedule an intake with yourself and fine-tune your timing, your "script," and your intake packet. Then you'll be ready to call friends, acquaintances, and other contacts and invite them to hire you as their coach!

Why use the Intake Meeting?

- To establish a coaching relationship and create a coaching contract with your clients.

- To provide the foundation for effective coaching.
- To clarify the client's present situation or clarify the client's current challenge and contract it with a "well-formed" goal that meets a set of requirements.

What does it do?

- Defines the role of the coach and the client
- Establishes the structure for the coaching process
- Provides opportunity to explore the client's strengths, talents, and values
- Defines the initial goals or the primary focus of the coaching process

How do I do it?

Set up a meeting to begin the coaching relationship. This meeting should allow enough time to cover the following topics:

1. Define the coaching relationship.
2. Discover the client's strengths, talents, and values.
3. Identify the client's overall goals and contrast them with the client's present situation. This identifies the gap to close for the client to achieve the success they want.
4. Pick one to three goals to use as a primary focus for the coaching.
5. Determine how the client wants to use you as a coach.
6. Decide how the client will be held accountable.

Here are some steps for developing a coach relationship:

1. Define the coaching relationship (see the section on The Coach Contract). This step defines the roles, clarifies expectations, and provides an opportunity to design the alliance that you will have with the client.
2. Discover the client's strengths, talents, and values. This is where you get to know the client, learn what is important, and what motivates him. It is worth the time to spend thirty minutes to an hour on this part of the intake. This will allow the client to shine and give you valuable information you can use in coaching him/her successfully.

Ask the client to prepare in advance a list of what he perceives as his personal strengths. This can include qualities and traits, special abilities and skills or other personal assets. Go over the list with him and encourage him to expand on it. Below are other categories to discuss:

VALUES AND CRITERIA

Ask the client what is important to him in general and in relation to the topical areas he wants to work on. A simple way to do this is to ask, "What do you want in a job (or relationship, or lifestyle, or _____?" If it is about career, the coach can ask, "What is important to you in your career?" Go through these criteria and ask how he knows when he is fulfilled.

MOTIVATION

An excellent tool at this point is the meta-program assessment (see the section on Meta-Programs). The skill of "Meta-Outcoming" will help to get to the client's deepest motivations. (see p. 84-86)

GOALS

Ask the client to describe long-term and short-term goals for coaching. Again, here we clarify the client's present situation or clarify the client's current challenge and contrast it with a "well-formed" goal, which is a goal that meets a set of requirements.

PERSONAL DEVELOPMENT

What skills and abilities would the client like to develop? What personal qualities or traits would he want to cultivate? What leaders or others might serve as role models or mentors to him?

Ask the client to pick one to three goals to use as a "primary focus" for the coaching process. Determine how the client wants to use you as a coach. Ask the client what she wants in you as a coach and how she would know that the coaching is working. Answers to these questions provide guidelines to use when coaching the client. Coaching is an evolving process, and these questions should be revisited periodically. Decide how the client wants to be held accountable.

A note on dual roles: In some cases, the coach may have a dual role with the client. For example, a supervisor may also provide coaching with an employee or work as a therapist. In such cases, it helps to make agreements about how the coach will "switch hats." This means that the coach cannot always truly function as a coach in the purest sense of the word (see the section on The Coach-Client Relationship). The coach needs to define clear markers for each role, which might include sitting in different chairs or using different rooms for each function. One way to do this is to use the metaphor of a hat. The coach tells the client when she is functioning as a therapist by "putting on the therapist hat" and when she is functioning as a coach by "putting on the coaching hat."

THE UNIVERSAL CYCLES OF CHANGE

What are The Universal Cycle of Change?

One way to think about coaching is that it helps the client manage change in his or her life in a conscious way. *The Universal Cycles of Change* is a description of the universal change process, and was developed primarily by Kristine Hallbom. It is especially useful for recognizing that change is inevitable, impossible to avoid, and that it has predictable cycles. If change is not considered or managed in a conscious way, it will still happen, but typically in a more chaotic way. One of the great benefits of coaching is that good coaching will facilitate more positive change and a smoother experience.

Why use The Universal Cycles of Change?

- To educate yourself and your client on the nature of change
- To assess where the client is at in the cycles of change
- To help the client recognize that change is inevitable and has an identifiable structure.
- To help the client manage change more effectively through maintaining the awareness of change.

What does it do?

- Identifies steps in the change process
- Offers a "diagnostic" and predictive tool for gauging client status in the change process
- Encourages decision-making and actions that are "ecological." This means that the actions are good for the person, don't limit other useful choices, and are good for the larger systems of which the client is part.

How do I use The Universal Cycles of Change?

The Universal Cycles of Change provides a frame for coaching. By recognizing that change will occur and respecting the cycles of change, you can coach someone to move through their lives in a better way. Here is a full description:

The Universal Cycles of Change is an ongoing process that's been happening in our Universe for about 13 billion years, since the beginning of time.

We have observed seven Universal Cycles of Change that occur in all living systems, such as plants, trees, stars, cells, and animals. You can also see these same cycles occurring in most non-living systems such as cars, houses, computers, and the economy.

The Universal Cycles of Change can also be found within all aspects of human life and behavior. They happen in marriages, business, with health, in families, with various states of mind and so on. We go through these cycles every day and every year of our life. Being aware of these cycles can help us to consciously create the kinds of life experiences that we want, and to bring forth the reality of our choice. The people who do well in life are naturally attuned to these cycles of change.

THE UNIVERSAL CYCLES OF CHANGE

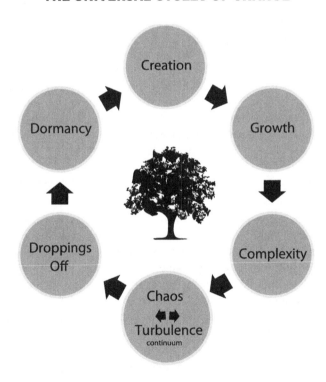

Here is a description of the seven phases of *The Universal Cycles of Change*:

1. **Creation**— This cycle is about new beginnings. Everything has a starting point, and typically that point begins with an idea, an action, or a blueprint. Some examples of this include starting a business, having a baby, investing in your first stock or fund, creating an idea for a book or a painting, building your first house, getting married, buying a new car, planting the seeds for a vegetable garden, or the Big Bang (the beginning of our universe as we know it).

2. **Growth**— When a system begins to grow and develop, it "self-organizes" as the initial creation begins to take shape or form. New patterns of behavior start to develop, and the system organizes itself around the original creation. For example, a new business develops a wonderful marketing plan, the stock that you've invested in begins to rise in price, the small tree that you've planted shows signs of growth, or your child speaks her first words and takes her first steps.

3. **Complexity to Maturity**— As a system takes shape and forms through continued growth, it becomes more complex until it reaches an optimal flow state or "steady state" and is operating at its best under current conditions. Some examples of a steady state are when things are going exceptionally well in your job, when an athlete enters into "the zone," when the tree that you have planted is sprouting beautiful green leaves, when your marriage is going incredibly well, when the car that you bought is running great, when the stock that you have invested in has made a big jump in the right direction, or when you're feeling good about yourself and everything in your life.

4. **Turbulence–Feedback**— When the system becomes too complex in its growth and development, problems occur and turbulence sets in. Turbulence is considered feedback from the environment that the system's complex state can no longer be supported—and that something has to be reorganized, changed, or dropped off. For example, you may have hired someone to work for you and that person isn't working out, you may start noticing some serious communication problems in your marriage that are affecting your individual health and well–being, the leaves on the tree that you planted begin changing color, you may have invested in a stock and it's starting to drop, you develop a minor physical symptom that is distracting, you notice signs of depression or dissatisfaction in your life, or your car starts making funny little sounds.

5. **Chaos**— This is when the system completely falls apart and chaos sets in. For example, the leaves on the tree turn brown and shrivel up, the troublesome employee acts out to the point that the overall welfare of the business is threatened, the stock you bought takes a huge drop, your marriage is completely falling apart, you get seriously ill, or the funny sound that your car was making turns into a loud sound and grey–blue smoke starts blowing out the tail pipe.

6. **Droppings Off and Reorganization**— Sometimes life becomes so complex that chaos sets in and you have to drop off something to help the system regain its overall balance. A snake shedding its skin or the leaves falling from the tree are examples of "dropping off." Even having to replace a part on your car is a form of dropping off or a type of reorganization. In order to move forward through a difficult life challenge, you often need to let go of a limiting belief, a dysfunctional relationship, make a change in behavior, or reorganize how you view the world in order to make space in your life to create something wonderfully new. All life forms in the universe, such as trees, snakes, and even stars, allow for this natural dropping off cycle to occur. Even non-living forms such as computers with animated trash bins, participate in droppings off. The purpose of the trash bin is to get rid of extra information on the hard drive because it takes up too much space.

7. **Meditation and Dormancy**— A system regains its balance by dropping something off and entering a dormancy phase in order to rejuvenate. This phase prepares the system to recycle back up to a new evolutionary level of creation. Just as the tree stands without leaves in the brisk cold winter, we sometimes need to go into a place of meditation and inner silence. It might be uncomfortable, but it can be very healing to quiet one's mind or to lay low for a while. When you give yourself plenty of "being time" to renew and rejuvenate, you can move forward with renewed energy and become creative again. You will have dropped off what was holding you back, yet you'll still have all the knowledge and wisdom that was gained from the whole experience. This sets the opportunity for a whole new cycle of creativity and growth. This is the final cycle in which the system regains its balance, which will allow it to recycle back up into…**Creation**. The system now has less mass, yet more energy because it contains all the learnings from the previous cycles.

A tree is a good practical example of the Universal Cycles of Change:

The first cycle a tree goes through is that of creation, which happens when a seed is planted. Then the tree grows—given that it has been provided with enough water and sunshine. Over time the tree reaches a steady state of maturity in which all of its leaves have blossomed with complete beauty. Then the autumn season sets in and the leaves begin to change color. They turn brown and drop to the ground. After this happens, the tree stands in dormancy without any leaves. But when spring comes around, the tree sprouts new leaves and the whole process of creation happens again.

Because all living systems eventually become too complex in their growth and development, they must have some kind of a dropping off to regain their balance. Trees do this all the time with their leaves. We can learn a lot by modeling trees. Have you ever been walking by a tree when its leaves are falling off and all of a sudden you hear the tree crying out, "Pleeeease, don't let my leaves fall off!" This never happens. The tree has mastered the art of dropping off and recycling back up to creation. Snakes are the same way when they shed their skin. We have never known of a snake to resist the process.

Interestingly, there is only one living system that does not allow itself to naturally go through this 13 billion-year-old process of change. This same system allows itself to stay stuck in turbulence and chaos for extended periods of time. This same system often resists dropping off what needs to be dropped off. Can you guess which system it is?

Human beings of course!

People represent the only living system in the universe that will allow themselves to stay stuck in turbulence and chaos. They are the only living systems that will not drop off whatever needs to be dropped in their life. We see this resistance happening frequently in relationships, career, and health.

One man shared an amazing realization that he had about *The Universal Cycles of Change*. This man had a teenage daughter with whom he had been unable to communicate effectively or happily for several years. After learning about The Universal Cycles of Change, he raised his hand and said,

"I finally understand why I have been having so many problems with my 17 year old daughter. In my mind I still think of her as a little child. I am now realizing that I need to 'drop off' my perception of her as a child and start treating her like a young adult. It makes complete sense to me why there has been so much turbulence and chaos in our relationship over the last two years."

In the case of the man who was having problems with his teenage daughter, it's not like he could just "drop off" the relationship with his child. His only option was to reorganize who he was within the context of the relationship. As soon as he stopped treating her like a little girl, and started perceiving her as a young adult, their relationship got better. The magic in what he did with his daughter can be found within the structure of his internal experience. He had an internal representation of her being a little girl. When he shifted that representation to her being an adult, then she started acting like an adult. By doing this, he was able to create an entirely new experience with his teenage daughter.

A woman described a powerful experience that she had with her children and *The Universal Cycles of Change* model. She said, "I just have to tell you about the funniest thing that happened to me last night. After I learned The Universal Cycles of Change model, I made the decision that I needed to 'drop off' the co–dependent relationship that I have with my five adult children," she said with excitement.

"Even though my children are grown up, they are all so needy. I felt like my life was all about them and there was no room for me. On my drive home last night, I set the intent to release the co–dependence that has been keeping me enmeshed with my children for so many years. After I got home, all 'chaos' broke loose. One by one, each child phoned me with some major crisis. One of my children's cars broke down, the other had just broken up with a boyfriend, another was having a bad day, and so on. The phone just kept ringing off the hook with their problems. I told each child one by one that they were responsible for themselves from now on and that they will need to solve their own problems." At this point in the story, she was glowing as she continued to say, "I just wanted to tell you that today is the beginning of the rest of my life. I am no longer co–dependent with my children and I can have my life back! I am returning to school, I am going to start painting again, and doing the kinds of things that make me happy. I am going to start living my life for me now, instead of for everyone else."

Often people are afraid to make changes because they are worried about throwing their lives into turbulence and chaos. In the case of the woman, she was concerned that her grown children would feel resentment towards her if she was not always fully present for them. Instead of being present for her children, she ended up resenting them because she wasn't able to live the life she wanted. Once she released her children from the co–dependent bonds, she was able to evolve into a new way of interacting with her children. And in doing so, she found that she could be more present for her children because she felt more spiritually fulfilled in her life.

As mentioned earlier, The Universal Cycles of Change influence all the areas of our lives. The primary life areas that they affect are:

* Romance and Love

* Career

* Health

* Family

* Money Matters

* Friends

* Spirituality

* Your Present State of Mind

You can use this for yourself and for clients assessing the current phase of the Universal Cycles of Change each area of life. If any areas are in turbulence or chaos, you may want to ask yourself, or help your client to identify, "What are some things that you need to drop off so that you can bring your life back into balance?"

It doesn't always have to be a dramatic dropping off. You can drop off something as simple as reading the morning newspaper or drinking diet coke every day. Categories to consider when thinking of things to drop off include: behaviors, beliefs, attitudes, ways of thinking, perceptions, habits, jobs, and relationships. Specific examples include: smoking, drinking too much alcohol, weight, television, coffee, unclear boundaries, frenetic busyness, old relationships that need to be updated, a troublesome employee, a toxic friendship, clutter, disorganization, grudges, anger, jealousy, unnecessary debt and unfinished business with people.

Our outer reality is a reflection of our inner reality. What nature can do for us is to serve as a perfect model for creating the life we want, as well as evolving to higher levels of personal and spiritual fulfillment. The answers to creating what we want in life can be found by becoming aware of *The Universal Cycles of Change* and applying them to all the various life areas. There is no reason why we can't harness the same kind of creative potential that exists within the seed of a plant or a star in our galaxy.

Barbara Walters was interviewing multi-billionaire Bill Gates, and asked him, "Now that you're the richest man in the world and you can have anything you desire, what more could you possibly want?"

Gates replied, "To never stop changing. Whatever I do today, will be considered history tomorrow. I have to make sure that I never stop changing; and that I am always creating."

Suggested Reading: *A Brief History of Everything* by Ken Wilber, *Complexity* by M. Mitchell Waldrop, *The Web of Life* by Fritjof Capra, *The Tree of Knowledge* by Humberto Maturana and Francisco Varela, *Chaos: Making A New Science* by James Gleick, *Steps to an Ecology of Mind* by Gregory Bateson, and *Psycho-Cybernetics* by Maxwell Maltz.

META-PROGRAMS

Meta-programs are subconscious mental-emotional filters that determine what you attend to, what you sort for, and what you respond to in life. These patterns identify how you process information and what motivates you to act. Meta-program profiling is especially helpful for coaching because meta-programs directly apply to what a person values or makes a priority.

These filters form your communication style and your preferences for how you interact with others and the world. Identifying your client's meta-programs provides a "profile" of the client's working style and motivational patterns. Once you know your client's meta-programs, you can tailor the coaching process to their unique ways and maximize the coaching impact.

The meta-programs as described below are adapted from the work of Roger Bailey, as well as from the work of Richard Bandler and Leslie Cameron-Bandler. For a full description of the Lab Profile distinctions, see the wonderful book, *Words that Change Minds*, by Shelley Rose Charvet. Another great resource is *Mindsonar*, an on-line Meta-Program tool developed by Jaap Hollander, of the Institute for Eclectic Psychology in Nijmegan, Holland.

It is important to note that these patterns are ***contextual***. They can and will be somewhat different for various contexts in life. In other words, the set of meta-programs that you use for work may be different than the set you might operate from in a relationship. Therefore, it is important to hold one context in mind when answering these questions.

Why use Meta-programs?

- To determine someone's thinking style
- To learn what motivates others
- To tailor your communication style to the client's style of processing input
- To deliver effective coaching assignments and encouraging client action toward goals

What does Meta-programming do?

- Helps you to get to know your client's thinking and motivation style.

- Identifies ways the client can communicate more effectively and helps you as the coach to improve your communication effectiveness with each client and their unique way of experiencing their world.

- Gives you the ability to make accurate predictions of how the client is likely to perform in specific contexts.

- Provides a powerful and precise way to identify what will motivate and de-motivate your client.

How is Meta-programming used?

You can use the meta-program profile in your intake interview. Explain that the profile serves as a tool for understanding your client and an aid in providing tailored coaching services. Many of the individual meta-program questions can also be asked as stand-alone questions at any time during the coaching process or to gather information about a context that is different than the one used in the intake. For instance, if the intake context is the job, you may ask later using the context of co-worker relationships or an intimate partner.

PART 1: THE META-PROGRAM PROCESS

First, we present the general steps to follow to determine the person's meta-programs. Then, we will analyze the specific items in the profile. A blank profile form can be found in the Appendix on page 136 of this book.

HERE ARE THE SEVEN STEPS FOR THE META-PROGRAM PROCESS:

1. Establish a context for the questions, such a job/career, co-worker relationships, friendship, spouse, etc. You will need to insert references to the context for certain questions and should make sure the client keeps the same context in mind throughout the interview.

2. Ask the questions using the exact words. The only addition or change is to adapt the content to the specific context. The questions have been carefully designed to get specific types of response. If you vary the wording, you may contaminate the responses and get invalid information.

3. Listen carefully to the client's responses. In some cases, you are listening for the form of the response in addition to the content. This means that you are attending to how the person responds (nonverbal patterns, tone of voice, etc) and sequencing of the response in addition to the actual words and meaning.

4. Some items offer a checklist for potential responses. Use the checklist to determine the client's style based on the response.

5. In some cases, you will note the exact key words/phrases used by the client. Make sure you use the client's key words and not synonyms or substitutes for them.

6. Keep in mind that for most, the meta-programs operate on a continuum. Virtually no one is all one way or another, but most people will skew to one side or the other in varying degrees. Meta-programs do not place someone in a category and we are not labeling a person. The profile reveals predictive unconscious drives and preferences.

7. With practice, you can complete a meta-program interview with someone conversationally and be able to make very accurate predictions about what environment, job, relationship etc. will offer the greatest chances for success.

PART 2: EXPLANATION OF PATTERNS:

Please look at the easy to use interview form in Appendix I on page 136. Keep in mind that people have access to the full range of patterns but tend to form preferred patterns, or meta-program sets, in specific contexts.

CRITERIA

Criteria are the words that a person (client) uses to describe what s/he considers to be important in a particular situation. These words are very meaningful to the client and elicit a strong feeling response. It is vital to recognize that the client's exact words are the ones to use. These words are deeply anchored to his/her experience whereas synonyms may not be. It is helpful to get five or six criteria words. Some of them will be very important to the client.

For example, a client had "top pay" as an important criterion in his work. When the words "top pay" were used in communicating with him, he lit up and became very attentive. Other synonyms, such as "good money," "high commission," "large remuneration," etc. were greeted with wariness on his part.

Questions to elicit criteria words:

1. What do you want in a (job, task, coach session, etc.)?
2. What's important to you in this context?
3. How is _____ of value to you?

When the client answers the questions, write down the criteria words he/she uses. Feed them back exactly as spoken and notice the positive response you get.

EVIDENCE

We use specific measures to determine if our criteria are met. For instance, if a criteria word for the context of a job is "challenge," then the person will sort for particular kinds of experiences judged as "challenging." Two people may both value "challenge" but have very different measures for fulfillment of challenge. One person may find an assignment requiring development of new procedures "challenging" while another may find it "challenging" to negotiate between people.

Questions to measure criteria:

1. How do you know when (name his/her criteria) is met?
2. What has to happen for (name his/her criteria) to be fulfilled for you?

When the client answers the questions, write down the response he/she gives, and you'll begin to understand what the client needs to feel motivated and interested. This is particularly valuable as a coach. Say the client wants "support" from you as a coach and measures "support" by "positive comments for successful action," and "consistently refocusing on goals." You can then offer support to the client in exactly the way the client needs it and knows it.

MOTIVATION TO TAKE ACTION

Are you motivated toward goals that you want to attain, or are you motivated by avoiding potential negative consequences or some combination of both?

- **Toward:** You are motivated to achieve or attain goals. You have trouble recognizing problems. You are good at managing priorities.

- **Away From:** You focus on what could go wrong, and what is going wrong now. You are motivated to fix problems and have trouble keeping focused on what you want to achieve.

Questions to determine motivation:

1. What does having that (name the client's criteria) do for you?
2. What's important about that (name the client's criteria?)
3. What's in it for you?

Responses indicating a "*Toward*" response: reach goal; obtain; have; get; achieve; reward.

Responses indicating an "*Away From Problems*" response: avoid; steer clear of; not have; get rid of; exclude; away from.

You'll hear both kinds of words if the person has a mixed response. You will want to use the balance of Toward and Away From words when trying to help the client get motivated.

DECISION SOURCE

"Who decides: me or someone else?"

- Internal: You are self-motivated in the chosen context; you might have difficulty accepting other's opinions and direction in a certain context. You "know best." When feedback is given, you might question the person giving it. You gather information and decide upon its usefulness. You know when you've done something well or not as a kind of inner certainty. You have a strong inner conviction about the right action to take. You might be hard to manage as you may not take direction well.

- External: You want, and in fact, require, other people's ideas, opinions, and feedback about how you are doing or what to do. You don't have clear inner standards for the best action to take. Without feedback from an external source, you might feel lost. You are likely to receive a suggestion as a command.

1. How do you know that you've done a good job?

    Internally referenced people will tell you they see it done properly, "It just feels right;" "I know;" or words to that effect. Externally referenced people will mention some kind of feedback from others. People who are both internal and external will mention both an inner knowing as well as external feedback.

Appropriate language to use for understanding and rapport:

- **Internal:** "What do you think? You're the only one to decide; Please consider…; It's up to you; Here's information so you can decide…."

- **External:** "Everyone knows…. You'll get helpful feedback….; This is well-respected information….; It has been approved by….; Experts say…"

PROCEDURES VS. OPTIONS

Do you need to create new ways to do things or do you prefer to follow established procedures?

- **Procedures Person:** You prefer to have rules or procedures to follow. You believe that there is a "right way" to do things in many situations. When you have no procedure to follow, you have no starting place. You might bumble around, not being clear on what to do. If you are a "procedures person," you will follow the recipe instead of inventing your own way.

- **Options Person:** If you have the options meta program, you'll want to develop new ways of doing things. To you, every situation is a new experience that offers a chance for developing a new way to resolve it. You are motivated by what needs to be done, not the way to do it. You are good at creating procedures for others to follow, but might have difficulty following them yourself. You will tend to break the rules. For example, you will not typically assemble something following the instructions, but will do it your own way.

"Why did you choose your present (name context; e.g. job) _____?"

Options People will give criteria. Procedures people will tell a story about how they got the job. Someone who is a mix of the two will give criteria and tell a story.

Appropriate language to use for understanding and rapport:

With Procedural Clients, speak in ordinals: "Do this first, then second, etc.; We need to do it the right way....;The steps to take...; Talk to them using the procedures s/he can use. For example, notice the difference in these two statements: "Call Phyllis for information." vs. a more procedural sentence "Pick up the phone and call Phyllis at (555) 555-5555 and ask how you can receive your free gift now." Talk about the "right way" to do something.

With Options Clients, talk about "what outcome is needed" not "how to do it." Suggest alternatives; possibilities, new way of doing it, etc.

MODE OF COMPARISON

- **Sameness:** You look for similarities, for what is the same. You have a very long time-line, and dislike change.

- **Sameness with Exception:** You notice what is the same; and then you will identify exceptions. You'll need a significant change about every 7 years.

- **Difference:** You notice what is different. You are more likely to mis-match what people say. You need significant change frequently and will often make major changes in the given context every 12-24 months. Note: in the work world, this might mean changing jobs or projects, taking on new responsibilities, etc. (In a marriage, a big change could mean traveling together, moving to a new home, having a child, etc.)

Question:

"What is the relationship between your (context) this year and (context) last year?" For example, "What is the relationship between your job this year and last year?"

Sameness Clients will respond by saying "It's the same."

Sameness with Exception Clients will say, "It's the same except I am working longer." Or, "It's better this year; I like my boss more," etc. Listen for words like more, better, improved, less, except, etc."

Difference Clients will say, "It is different." Or "It's all new," or other words that speak to differences.

CONVINCER

What type of evidence does a person need to gather in order to start the process of being convinced? This has two parts, "channel" and "mode."

Channel

- **See:** Visual evidence: you need to see the behavior, action or product. (Or you need to see a representation of it, like a diagram or a picture.)
- **Read:** You are convinced because something is in writing. When you have read it, you begin to become convinced.
- **Hear:** You need to be told about something or hear people talk about it.
- **Do:** You have to actually do something, or actively do something with another person.

Question:

How do you know when someone is doing a good job?

Responses will be a version of: "I see it, or heard about it, or I read it, or I tried it out."

Appropriate language to use for understanding and rapport:

Match their response by matching their language patterns and the sensory channel they answer with.

- **Number of Examples:** You need to witness or experience an action, service, skill, or product a certain number of times to be convinced or learn something.

- **Automatic:** You will make assumptions that something is the case with only a little information. You may jump to conclusions and/or give the benefit of the doubt. Once you have made up your mind, you do not easily change it.

- **Consistent:** You need to reevaluate every time. You are never completely convinced.

- **Period of Time:** You need to gather information over time before you are sure of something.

ACTION LEVEL

Does this person take initiative or wait for others? As with other patterns, this may change by context. A person may be proactive in a situation that s/he is familiar with and reactive in one where it is unclear what action to take, the safety of the situation, etc. For example, one shy client was proactive in situations where he knew all the others involved and knew he was liked. He became reactive in situation dealing with strangers until he thought they felt ok about him. Then he would gradually get more proactive.

- **Proactive:** You take initiative. At the extreme, you "go for it" with little or no planning. You are motivated by taking action and demotivated if you have to wait.

Appropriate language to use for understanding and rapport:

"Do it; Go for it; Make it happen; Now; Get it done; Don't wait..."

- **Reactive:** You wait for others to take action or gather information before moving ahead. You are motivated to bide your time, analyze the situation, "don't fix it if it isn't broken," etc. You will do well in jobs where people come to you and you can react to their needs rather than having to initiate the action.

Appropriate language to use for understanding and rapport:

Evaluate; understand; think about; wait; study; ponder; might; could;

would; assess.

There isn't a specific question for this pattern – listen to the language used by the client. Proactive people will use words like "go for it, just do it, etc." The proactive pattern uses language that is active and direct with clear subject and action: "I ran the crew." "I will write the report." Reactive people will say, words like, "Wait, check it out first, Think about it; consider it. etc." The reactive language pattern uses passive voice and often omits reference to the agent: "The crew was organized." Or with more words between the subject and the verb: "I'll think about what might be written in the report."

BIG PICTURE VS. DETAIL ORIENTATION

Does the person pay attention to the big picture or details – in other words does s/he literally notice the forest or the trees?

- **Specific (Focus on the Details):** You deal well with small chunks of information and may have trouble summarizing or seeing the bigger picture. You will tend to be sequential and linear in your thinking and descriptions. You will give lots of information and detail and will expect detailed descriptions from others. You are effective where details must be handled. You give lots of information as you talk about something.

- **General (Focus on the Big Picture):** You tend to think conceptually and see things in an overview. You will use general statements, talk in broad categories, and offer brief summaries, and likely use fewer words. You'll become frustrated if forced to deal with or listen to lots of details for lengthy periods.

Question:

Tell me about a work experience that you really enjoyed.

If the client gives lots of information she is more likely oriented toward detail. If the client gives little information or a broad summary, she is more likely to be a big picture person.

Appropriate language to use for understanding and rapport:

With the Detail Oriented Person (Specific) used words that imply detail:

"exactly"; "precisely"; "particularly"; "specifically;" and give lots of details to express, explain, or support a topic or point.

With the Big Picture (General) person, use words that imply summary or generalization: "The important thing is"; "In general"; "The bottom line is..."; "Here is the big picture" etc. And give visions, goals, summaries, or broad strokes of information.

ATTENTION DIRECTION

Do you naturally pay attention to the nonverbal behavior of others, or to your own internal experiences?

There is no specific question for this pattern. It can be identified through observation of the client's non-verbal behavior.

- **Self:** You tend not to show your feelings and may have a flat affect. You tend to be more aware of yourself and your needs than those of others. You pay attention to the words said rather than the nonverbal cues offered by others and may miss some messages people send you. Interpersonal communication skills are not your strong point.

Appropriate language to use for understanding and rapport:

Keep the communication focused on content; and match their criteria.

- **Other:** You respond immediately to other's communications or behaviors and are adept at hearing voice tone shifts and noticing body language. You are compelled to respond to others and tend to be more animated.

Appropriate language to use for understanding and rapport:

Increase the depth of rapport by matching or acknowledging affect.

TIME ORIENTATION

What time reference does the person typically use? The past? The present? The future?

- **Past oriented:** You are focused on the past. You can access past experiences easily. You can find it difficult to deal with change and will not be good at planning. You may seem critical of new ideas and proposals. ("We tried that 5 years ago and it didn't work.")

- **Present oriented:** You are oriented to now. You sense your feelings clearly. You will tend to be "in the moment" and get caught up in what you are doing at any given time. At the extreme, you can get lost in the moment and not consider the past or the future.

- **Future oriented:** You are good at planning the future. At the extreme, you might not notice what is happening now, and may not learn from past errors.

Appropriate language to use for understanding and rapport:

Use the same time references.

STYLE

What kind of environment allows the person to be most productive: working alone, with others around, or sharing responsibility?

- **Independent:** You like to work alone and have responsibility for your results. The quality of your work can suffer if you have to share decisions or work with others as a part of a team.

- **Proximity:** You want to have the responsibility for the project, but like to have others involved or around, "in proximity." Productivity will fall if you have to share responsibility as a member of a team, or if you have to work all by yourself. You will be a good project manager.

- **Co-operative:** You like being a part of the team and want to share responsibility with others. You may have trouble with deadlines if you have to work alone. As a manager you will want to do things with your employees.

Question:

Tell me about an experience that was (criteria) and what did you like about it?

In the response, listen for whether the client just talks about what he did (independent), about himself and others ("I helped my direct report to establish new goals."), or if the client says "We..." or "Us..." etc.

Appropriate language to use for understanding and rapport:

With an Independent Client: You will do it yourself; by yourself; you have the responsibility; you'll work independently; you're the one, no one will bother you.

With a Proximity Client: You'll be in working with others, but have the ultimate responsibility; you'll be in charge; you are the lead person, etc.

With a Co-operative Client: Us; we; all together; teamwork; shared responsibility; let's, etc.

META-PROGRAM CASE STUDY

Rebecca worked in the Human Resources/Training department of a large corporation. HR staff offered some limited coaching services to the managers and employees. She had been coaching Eric, a middle manager, but the coaching was going slowly and Rebecca felt that she was missing something important about Eric. She learned the meta-program profiling tool and applied it with Eric both to learn the tool and to improve her coaching with Eric.

Rebecca immediately learned her style of coaching was mismatched with Eric in three ways:

First, Eric was very options oriented while Rebecca was procedural. So, she kept asking him questions about specific steps, which Eric seemed to "avoid." She realized he wasn't really avoiding, he just did not think that way. She started using options language and immediately found that Eric responded more positively.

Second, Eric's working style was "co-operative," and he needed to work with others. She had missed this about him and found Eric had failed to follow-through on her suggestions for assignments. She realized that she had been giving him individual assignments, primarily self-reflective exercises that he could do on his own. She shifted to giving assignments that involved acting with others and found that Eric was more excited about the assignments and more likely to complete them.

Third, she recognized that Eric was motivated by external reasons and knew that he wanted to please her and others. She could see how this had resulted in some problems in the coaching process—Eric wanted answers and she had refused to give them to him. She changed the direction of assignments, suggesting he find mentors, read books and locate external authorities to help him address specific issues.

Rebecca found many other patterns that served her in coaching Eric more effectively. She found that she could match his criteria and evidence as a powerful tool for understanding his motivation and for coaching him on issues. She also used his pattern of going from general to specific to sequence coaching topics and found the whole process went more smoothly. Once she made the shift from using her preferred patterns to match Eric's style, the coaching picked up momentum, increasing her confidence and improving her effectiveness as a coach and accelerating measurable results with Eric.

Coaching 101: The Basics

COMMUNICATION BLOCKERS

What are Communication Blockers?

These communication blockers are responses typically intended to be helpful but which often don't work and can actually discourage good communications. Thomas Gordon (the developer of Leader Effectiveness Training) (1977) lists twelve such responses, which follow below.

Why use them?

Exploring these common communication mistakes will make you aware of them and help you to avoid them.

How do I recognize Communication Blockers?

The goal here is to sensitize you to the problem state. All of us slip into these problem communications occasionally. Imagine how you would feel if you were a client and getting responses like these:

- **Solution Giving:** "Here is what you need to do to solve your problem."
- **Commanding:** "Just stop talking so that I can give you my opinion!"
- **Warning:** "If you miss another session, I won't work with you as a coach."
- **Moralizing:** "You should be more gentle with yourself; being critical of yourself or others is not very useful."
- **Lecturing:** "Research shows that a state of uncertainty is helpful to learning new things in a coach context."
- **Advising:** "Why don't you go and talk directly to the person that you are having trouble with. Getting it out in the open will help you to feel better."

- **Judgments:** "I don't think that what you are planning to do is a good idea."

- **Blaming:** "There's no one to blame but you for the problem you're having, is there?"

- **Name Calling:** "I agree with you that your boss sounds like a complete idiot."

- **Analyzing:** "I'm sure I was quite clear. Perhaps we should work on your listening skills."

- **Denying:** "Your boss isn't angry with you, it's just the way he comes across."

- **Praising:** "Good boy for making an attempt to understand it. Trying is the important thing."

- **Reassuring:** "You poor old thing. Hang in there though. Life's bound get easier over time."

- **Distracting:** "Maybe we should change the subject so that we can get some distance from the problem."

- **Interrogating:** "What were you doing when it happened?" "Why weren't the other staff involved?" "What did your assistant do?"

- **Questioning the client's judgment:** "Do you always have trouble with that employee?" "Is there something else that you could do to communicate with him?" "Have you tried a number of different ways to get through to him?" "Is he having personal problems that you don't know about?"

It can be helpful for the coach to recognize which of these communication blockers he or she might be in the habit of using and to avoid them. None of them has a place in coaching and will most likely shut the client down when the goal is to "bring out the best in the client."

COACHING AND NONVERBAL COMMUNICA-
TION

Why use nonverbal communication?

To dramatically improve your communications and have more conscious control over your own internal experience.

What is it?

We are always a part of a system. You are a system made up of a number of other systems: you have a circulatory system, a digestive system, a musculo-skeletal system, a nervous system, and so on. Whenever one of these systems is impacted, the relationships between all of the systems shift. For example, when you alter your posture in certain ways, you will change the way that you see, hear, and come across to others.

How do I do it?

Nonverbal communication is highly significant in overall communication. To really understand this, try the following experiment:

1. Scoot back on your chair so that your posterior is touching the back of the chair and you are sitting upright. Lean forward slightly and imagine that you are in a conversation with someone. Notice your state. Now, scoot forward in your chair about six inches, then sit back and rest your upper back on the chair. Notice how your state changes. Move back and forth from these two positions, noticing the angle of your vision and what shifts in your consciousness.

2. Leaning more forward—more focused, connected. Leaning back—more detached, looking more at the big picture. Notice the change in the angle of your vision.

3. Now try this: Stand up with your feet about hip width apart. Notice the angle of your vision. Then move your toes out and heels toward each other slightly. Notice the visual shift; then move your feet so that they are straight (really straight, like railroad tracks) and again, notice the difference in the angle of your vision.

4. Now go for a walk, first with your feet straight, then with them open. Check out the difference in your attitude and what you attend to when "straight" versus "open." Most people experience a

profound difference. With your feet straight, you are most likely in a state of purposeful attention. When your feet are open, you slow down, look around more, and feel more laid back.

Consider the implications for coaching. As you change your posture, profound communication differences arise in your ability to gain connection and understanding. Keep in mind that one posture or stance is not better than another but that each simply produces a different outcome.

SYSTEMIC COMMUNICATIONS

We have explored what happens to a system comprised of two people in communication and discovered subtle shifts in body posture create dramatically different experiences in communication and connection. Find a colleague and try this process in actual experience: merely guessing what might happen won't give you the same discoveries as actually doing it.

COMMUNICATION EXERCISE

In your pair, appoint two roles:

1. An employee who is coming to work late.
2. A supervisor who gives feedback about this to the employee.

The employee doesn't respond but notes how she receives the feedback.

☞ **Round One:** Supervisor gives the feedback "face to face"

When the feedback is given, notice how the supervisor delivers the feedback and the way that it is received by the employee. Explore the distance between supervisor and employee and the angle of the supervisor's feet (straight versus toes turned out).

In most Western cultures, people will communicate with each other face to face and about an arm's length apart. Start by giving the feedback from an arm's length away.

The supervisor should experiment by splaying his feet slightly while giving the feedback, then giving it with his feet straight. Notice the response received and the way that it feels to be the supervisor with each of these variations. Now step closer and express the feedback from fifteen inches away. Again, take a moment to notice the feelings and any shifts in tone of voice, selection of words, or other behaviors.

Now move apart by seven or eight feet. Deliver the feedback and note the changes on the part of both people.

☞ **Round Two:** Supervisor gives the feedback "to the employee's side"

Give the feedback about coming to work late while standing at a three-quarters angle from your partner. Notice what shifts in the analogue of the supervisor and employee. (Analogue refers to the voice tone and tempo, body language, muscle tension, and autonomic changes that occur in a communication, in other words, all the signals except content.) Explore the distance. Notice the differences when you get closer when you are to the side of the employee from when you got closer on the front. How does it change the interaction? Also notice how you can stay more connected when you are farther away.

NOTE Regarding Touch: We are not advocating touch, which can be a very sensitive matter, especially in the workplace, and should only be done appropriately and respectfully. For some, all touch is off-limits, either culturally, such as touch between a man and an unmarried woman in some cultures, or personally. You should always honor such boundaries. For the exercise, ask if it is OK to touch before doing so.

Now add touch. Make it a gentle, momentary touch on the arm as you would if someone were blocking your way at the supermarket. You might lean over, barely touch her and say, "Excuse me." Pay attention to how your analogue changes with the touch. Note how the employee responds. Years ago, a study on honesty was conducted, and it was found that people tended to be more honest when they were appropriately touched. Of course, touching people does not cause them to be more honest, but touch creates a different relationship. In the supervisor-employee experiment, notice that there will be a softening of the voice and a different countenance on the part of the supervisor.

Last, try giving feedback on the left side of the person, and then deliver it from their right side. Notice the difference in response. Also attend to your feelings as supervisor. The employee is probably looking at you differently from one side or the other.

When we (Tim Hallbom and Suzi Smith, another coach and NLP Trainer) first discovered this, we thought it had to do with handedness or a dominant side. However, our research showed that about half the people prefer feedback on their right side and about half on the left. We discovered that side preference has to do with self-talk. Most people have a critical voice that they hear in their mind that was "installed" while they were growing up. It is an interjected voice that they acquired from a significant other, usually Dad or Mom. These critical voices typically seem to come from one side or the other. We don't like criticism that comes from the side on which we criticize ourselves.

The point of these exercises is to notice how profoundly relationships can change by changing the spatial relationship between the listener and the speaker. As a rule, the coach should be "to the side of" the client. Talking straight on is good for an informal chat but not for the serious work of coaching when you want to be unobtrusive and allow the client space to process her thoughts. Try these experiments in real-life situations and you will learn some very powerful communication skills.

ACTIVE LISTENING AND BACKTRACKING

What is Active Listening and Backtracking?

Great coaches are highly effective listeners. Developing and refining the ability to feedback what you hear from your client is a key listening skill. "Active Listening," a well-known skill, suggests the listener feedback the speaker's content by paraphrasing what the speaker said. "Backtracking" is a special kind of active listening where the coach feeds back what clients said using the client's key words. When you use the client's own words you will be communicating in the same way that they are thinking.

Why use it?

Backtracking is useful for:

- Gaining rapport through matching the content and the process words of the client's statements.

- Making sure you understand the client's statements.

- Giving you time to think about what you're going to say next.

- Increasing your attentiveness as a listener so you can repeat parts of it back.

- Providing the client with confirmation that you are really listening.

- Checking the speaker's congruence. Sometimes a person realizes an expressed desire or concern isn't really it only after hearing it repeated back. But even more important, the client's body will demonstrate congruence and reveal the client's level of genuine commitment. Notice whether the client responds to the key words as you backtrack with a "whole body yes. " For example, the client says, "I want X (key word/phrase)." The coach can watch for congruence when feeding back, "Oh, so you want X (same key word/ phrase)." If the client nods affirmatively or clearly signals "yes," it is likely correct. If the client has hesitation or expresses doubt, it might be worth exploring more deeply.

How to do it:

Listen attentively and feed back what the client says, being sure to use their key words (predicates).

☞ Example:

Client: "I am <u>worried</u> about my <u>role</u> in the XYZ project."

Coach: "So you are worried about your role in the XYZ project – what is it specifically that concerns you?"

Client: "I am not really <u>clear</u> about how much <u>authority</u> I have for making spending decisions."

Coach: "So, you want clarity about your level of authority for spending decisions?"

Client: "Yes. I get really <u>stuck</u> when I <u>worry</u> about <u>making decisions</u> that my boss won't later <u>support</u>."

Coach: "OK, what might you do to clarify your level of authority in making decisions your boss can support so that you don't get stuck in this way?

...And so on

PERCEPTUAL POSITIONS

What are Perceptual Positions?

Helping the client adopt different perceptual positions and ways of thinking is a key element of coaching. This process is especially helpful when coaching around relationship dynamics, whether in the workplace, family life, or social situations, especially if there is a need to cooperate in some way, or if conflicts arise, or when a deeper understanding of the situation would be useful. Developing the ability to shift between three primary perceptual position can provide powerful insights and offer new choices that can serve all parties.

There are three perceptual positions: Self, Other, and Observer:

1. **Self** – The self position uses the pronoun I—"I woke up in the morning and I went to school." It is an associated position meaning you're in your body, you're hearing and seeing things through your own experience, and you are accessing your own neurology. It's your point of view, which is, of course, colored by all your unique beliefs, attitudes, experiences, limitations, and knowledge.

2. **Other** - In the "other" position, you consider a situation as if you are the other person—looking at it through their eyes, adopting their physiology, personal values, and personal history (as far as you are informed). The more complete the shift, the more information you'll gather. It's like saying, "If I were you, how would I think about this?" You "become" another person and take on his perspective.

3. **Observer** - In the "observer" position, you consider a situation from a neutral, third-party point of view, seeing yourself and the others involved as if from the outside. This is an objective point of view where you take a detached, disassociated perspective. In this position, you use the pronouns "she," "he," and "they" (even when talking about yourself). When you step back from Self and consider "the big picture" of something, you are in a "Meta-position" above or outside of the situation as a neutral observer with no feelings or opinions about it.

PERCEPTUAL POSITIONS EXERCISE

Imagine that you're going parachuting. Initially, you are in a position on the ground, watching the airplane go by and observing people as they jump out of the plane. After they fall for a little bit, the parachute opens, and you see them float down. Imagine seeing someone who looks like you doing that and notice what it feels like.

Now imagine that you're actually in the airplane. While flying along, the doors open so that you're looking out at the sky around you and the ground far below. You can feel the breeze blowing in through the open door. There are a few people ahead of you and you watch them step up to the edge, jump out of the plane and quickly start disappearing. Now it's your turn. You look way down to the ground, twelve thousand feet below, as you grip on to the handles. You hear the roar of the motors and feel the vibration of the airplane, before releasing your hold and you jump, and you are falling, falling wildly and rapidly, the distant ground growing closer as you continue to dive through the air, the wind rippling your face. You reach over, feeling the added effort of the move, and pull the string—then you feel the parachute open, the sudden catch, stopping your descent for a second, and then you float, held up by the ropes as the ground draws near and your feet ready for touchdown.

The first narrative describes the "observer position;" the second one, the "self" position. What's the difference in your experience? In the first story, there's not much feeling. You only have the detached, objective feelings of the Observer, not those of the participant (Self).

People remember events from different perspectives. Take a minute and think of a few positive experience that you've had in the last few months. They could be something important that you did with someone else, a personal success at work, or a fun evening that you spent with a friend. How do you remember it? You may remember it by being in it, looking out of your own eyes. You might remember the experience from the perspective of "watching yourself." You may even flip back and forth between viewpoints.

Now think of a negative experience that happened in the last few months. Don't choose the worst event of your life; recall a minor event such as when someone was rude or you lost something. Notice how you think about it. How do you recall that negative experience? Is it from an associated (seeing out of your own eyes) or disassociated (seeing yourself as if from outside) state? From a disassociated place, you'll likely think, "That happened, but it's in the past." If you remember it from an associated state, you will likely feel the negative feelings all over again.

Do you know people who are always negative, grouchy, unfriendly or depressed? They may be continually accessing their negative experiences from the Self position instead of from Observer.

It's useful to start noticing these perspectives and to realize that you have a choice about them. When you're in Self position, you're going to have access to your passion and feelings. When you're in the Observer position, you're going to be detached. They're both useful positions for different situations.

Exceptional actors often go to the Other Position with their character and mentally become the character. A great example of perceptual positions is the work of actor Dustin Hoffman. When he starred in the film *Rain Man*, he played an autistic savant. He created the character from several sources but in particular by studying a man named Kim Peek, who has been referred to as "The Real Rain Man." Peek has some remarkable abilities, as is depicted in the film. Hoffman studied him for two months. He learned how to "go

Other" with Kim Peek so precisely that he moved and sounded just like him.

About fifteen years ago, a psychological association tried to pass a law that basically proposed that "only psychologists could do psychological interventions to affect change with other people." The legislative bill stated that psychology consists of anything you do that induces change in someone else, whether you get paid for it or not. Certain professions were exempt, such as teachers, clergy, licensed social workers, psychiatrists, and doctors, but if you think about it, the bill could impact the field of training, managing, swimming instruction, or just about anything. For example, if you go to a training, you're learning new skills. Imagine that you went to a Spanish class and just as you said, "Hola, que tal?" the police could nab your instructors and throw them into jail.

What Perceptual Position had the psychological association taken? It was looking at "psychology" only from its point of view; it never considered all the other points of view. One of the larger groups that strongly opposed the bill was a program for the elderly, which was completely staffed by volunteers. They weren't licensed therapists, they were all volunteers, but the bill would have shut down all those programs for senior citizens in the state. Fortunately, the bill didn't pass.

This is an example of looking at an issue from only one perspective. Wise decision making involves inclusion of various perspectives. Passionate commitment is one thing, wisdom is another. Vincent van Gogh was passionate about his painting and excelled in his art. On the other hand, he didn't have wisdom: it probably wasn't wise to chop off his ear and give it to someone as a pick-up line.

Gandhi was once asked how he thought he could negotiate with England. He didn't have any money or power, compared to the huge government that controlled his country. Gandhi said, "First, I'm going to consider the negotiation from the point of view of truth." Gandhi was a person who devoted his life to finding his truth (his autobiography is called *My Experiments with Truth*). He was trying to find out what was true in the world and how to learn from that space. Where would his truth be? It would originate in his own self perspective.

Gandhi said, "I'm going to consider truth from the point of view of the Viceroy, the Untouchables, the Hindus, and the Muslims." A woman who lived in the ashram with him said that before the negotiation with the Viceroy of England, he walked around the room moving his hands like the Viceroy and acting like the Viceroy. He was doing what Dustin Hoffman does: becoming the other person so that he could get the other person's point of view. He became Nehru, and then Ali, who was the head of the Muslim Congress. Then Gandhi said, "I'll step back and look at this situation from the eyes of the world."

Part of his negotiation strategy was to take clean, clear perceptual positions and rehearse the other person's point of view so that he could make a much wider range of wise decisions. Coming to a negotiation from only one perspective is limiting; coming from a wide variety of perspectives is very powerful.

Jonas Salk, who discovered the vaccine for polio, is reported to have said, "What would I do as a virus? If I were these virus cells, what would I do?" He "became" the virus, and that perspective gave him new insight.

Einstein didn't come up with the theory of relativity by wearing a white smock and writing a million formulas on a blackboard. He said to himself, "What would it be like to be on the end of a light beam, shooting ahead in space? What if I were on the end of a light beam and I held a mirror in front of me—would I be able to see my face, or would the light not yet be there?" He came up with original ideas by taking different perceptual positions.

What do Perceptual Positions accomplish?

1. They provide a way to separate one's own opinions and beliefs from others

2. They help access resources from the client's life experiences.

3. They offer perspectives to discover creative solutions to challenges.

How do I use Perceptual Positions?

☞ Exercise I

1. Take a moment and remember an argument or a situation where you were intimidated, or a situation where someone did some be-

havior that resulted in hurt feelings on your part. Choose a situation that is mild to moderately unpleasant.

2.   Remember the situation by stepping back into it - see, hear, and feel what occurred from your own point of view (Self). Identify your feelings and your understanding of the experience.

3.   Float up and out to a neutral position (watching from above or from the side). Watch yourself and the other person in detail (Observer). Notice how both the other person and the "you over there" sounds look, move, breathe, and so on. Consider any information you have about the other person's values, beliefs, personal history, and how the context and experiences immediately prior to the event you're remembering might be perceived.

4.   Float down into the other person, becoming her as fully as possible, adapting her physiology, perspective, history, and so on. Replay the situation in your mind (fully and completely) from her point of view (Other).

5.   Float up and off to the side. Watch the interaction again noticing how both the other person and the "you over there" sound, look, move, breathe, and so on but now with the added information of from both perspectives: Self and Other.

6.   Return to Self. Review the situation again completely. Signal to B when you're finished.

Answer the following questions:

- "What has changed for you in relation to this memory?"
- "Which was easiest to do?
- "How might this be valuable in your life? Your work?"

This can be a very useful process to guide a client through when he is confused or upset about another person's or group's behavior.

☞ Exercise II

With partners, appoint three roles: **A**, **B**, and **C**.

A tells a story. **B** listens for two minutes in each Perceptual Position without interacting with **A** (**B** spends two minutes respectively in Self, Observer, and Other positions). **C** observes both **A** and **B** with particular attention on cues to indicate when **B** shifts perceptual position, and the physiological and voice tone shifts in **A** that correlate with **B**'s shifts. All parties notice the effect that **B**'s shifts in Perceptual Positions have on **A**. The group shares perceptions of the implications of each position on the communication.

PERCEPTUAL POSITION CASE STUDY

Max complained that he had an ongoing problem with a coworker. During a coach session, Max complained that he just had a run-in with co-worker who was "defensive" when he gave her some necessary feedback and that this was an ongoing problem with her.

The coach first had him relive the experience from the Self position. Max reiterated how angry he felt when he was being "attacked" by this person. Next, the coach had him step back to the Observer position and watch the experience as if from the outside. Here, Max could detach from himself and gather information without getting caught up in his feelings. He could observe the interaction as a behavioral exchange. The coach then asked Max to imagined actually being the coworker: to stand the way that she did and do his honest best to take on her viewpoint and life experiences as far as he knew them. He experienced the event through her eyes.

When he returned to the Self position, after having "stepped into her" as literally as he could, he realized how his style came across as intimidating to her. He thought through how he could present information more effectively with her in the future and in a way that would not intimidate her. Max noted that the process gave him powerful insight into his own behavior and the impact it might have on others. The coaching session then focused on strategies to deal with the co-worker that he could also apply in lots of situations in life. Max reported that he felt empowered because it gave him a way out "playing a blame game" and being a victim.

OPEN QUESTIONS

Why use open questions?

A primary skill of effective coaching is asking good questions. Open questions, as opposed to closed questions, generally serve better in helping the client articulate thoughts and feelings, clarify issues, dig deeper for creative responses, and find their own solutions.

What are they?

These are questions that cannot be answered by a simple "yes," "no," or by a single word or number. They invite the person to talk further, and they direct the client's attention to a specific aspect of what has been said. Open questions can ask for more sensory-specific information. For example, an open question in response to a client's claim that "My friend is always putting me down!" might be, "How, specifically, does your friend put you down?" or "When, specifically, does she do that?"

How do I use open questions?

Open questions that start with "how" elicit better information than those which start with "why." "Why" questions tend to create defensive responses and elicit excuses, justifications, and explanations. The following exercise will help get you to think about how to structure your questions effectively.

Open questions can ask for more information about the person's desired outcome. "How would you know if this problem was solved?" or "What needs to be different for you to feel good about this?"

Open Questions Examples

1. **A client has been discussing his frustration about the way his previous coach worked with him, which included offering lots of advice.**

   - Ineffective closed question: "Did you tell this to your coach?"
   - Possible open question: "Having had that experience, what do you want in a coaching relationship now?"
   - Write another useful open question:

2. **A client has been telling you that she finds her work a challenge because the company won't provide training.**

    ■ Ineffective closed question: "Are you upset about that?"

    ■ Possible open question: "What skills do you feel you need or want to improve?"

    ■ Write another useful open question:

3. **A client expresses feelings of resentment about how she was treated by someone at a party.**

    ■ Ineffective closed question: "Did you speak up about this?"

    ■ Possible open question: "What is important about this to you now?"

    ■ Write another useful open question:

4. **A client has just explained that she hated sports as a teenager.**

    ■ Ineffective closed question: "Do you hate sports now?"

    ■ Possible open question: "How do you think that affects you now?"

    ■ Write another useful open question:

5. **An unemployed friend tells you he is trying to get a job at a place where you have a contact.**

    ■ Ineffective closed question: "Do you want me to ask the boss about it?"

    ■ Possible open question: "How can I help you with that?"

    ■ Write another useful open question:

6. **A client explains that she didn't get the promotion she wanted so she's applied for a job at another company.**

    ■ Ineffective closed question: "Do you want to work for them?"

    ■ Possible open question: "Why do you think that they didn't hire you and what might you do next time you apply for a job that you want?"

    ■ Write another useful open question:

7. **A client begins to cry about a situation that has arisen.**

    ■ Ineffective closed question: "Are you okay?"

    ■ Possible open question: After acknowledging that it is ok for the client to have these feelings, you can ask, "Now that you are letting your feelings out, how do you want to deal with this situation?"

- Write another useful open question:

8. **A client discusses his feelings of depression after he loses his job.**

   - Ineffective closed question: "If you could be the way you wanted, would you let go of those sad feelings?"

   - Possible open question: "You've lost your job, and that's tough, what is your next move?"

   - Write another useful open question

VERY USEFUL COACH QUESTIONS: THE META-MODEL

A great many problems in life result from poor communication with others. The meta-model is an excellent tool because it works to clarify ad specify communication when it is necessary and appropriate. It provides a method for dealing with what is missing, distorted, or over-generalized in thinking and communicating. The meta-model offers some very powerful questions for coaching and provides a framework for knowing when to ask the right question.

What is The Meta Model?

Many of the NLP techniques used in coaching originated with the Meta Model. John Grinder and Richard Bandler developed the Meta Model to identify and clarify classes of language patterns in order to improve communication. Bandler and Grinder began this process by modeling change experts Virginia Satir (the originator of family therapy), Milton Erickson (a famous psychiatrist), and Fritz Perls (the developer of Gestalt therapy), who all used Meta Model inquiries intuitively yet with great skill.

One of the basic presuppositions of NLP is expressed in the metaphor that "the map is not the territory." Maps are useful because they have a similarity to the terrain they depict, but any map will be a limited and incomplete representation of the terrain. The external world, what may be called "reality," is like the terrain. At any given moment, we are bombarded with billions of bits of information. But we can only process a small portion of what we receive from the world. Without our brain's ability to filter information by deleting, distorting, and generalizing input, we would be overwhelmed. We unconsciously create mental models or maps that serve this filtering function. Our maps select what to attend to, what is important, what events mean, how the world works, etc. We then use these "maps" of the world to guide our behavior and negotiate life.

As a good communicator, it is useful to understand another's "map of the world," and the Meta Model provides techniques for gathering this information. Our "maps" either empower us or limit us, so our goal is to increase the chances that language will empower us.

What does the Meta Model do?

- Helps to clarify the thoughts of the speaker for better understanding.
- Uses language to draw out a person's model of the world, which is below the surface of thinking.
- Creates change in a person's experience by expanding her model of the world and creating more options for thinking, deciding, and acting.

Every word is an anchor for a deeper and often richer set of meanings. For each listener, the same set of words will create different ideas and images depending upon his experience. For instance, what literal representation comes to your mind when I say: "She showed me something." Who is she? What is she showing me? How is she showing it to me? You might ask, "Who is showing you what and how are they showing you?" I could then respond, "My dog Penny showed me her puppy by carrying it to me in her mouth."

The Meta Model distinctions fall into three identifying sets:

1. **Gathering Information (Deletions)**
   - Noun Deletions (who, what, which, where, or when is left out)
   - Comparative Deletions (there is an implied comparison)
   - Lack of Referential Index (unspecified person, place, or thing)
   - Unspecified Processes (the "how" of it is unclear—the process is vague)
   - Nominalizations (an active process is mentally changed into a static thing)

2. **Limits of the Speaker's Model (Generalizations)**

   ■ Universal Quantifiers: Absolutes (all, always, never, nobody, and so on)

   ■ Modal Operators of Necessity (should, must have to, and so on)

   ■ Modal Operators of Impossibility (can't, impossible, not able to, and so on)

   ■ Lost Performatives (over-generalized judgments)

3. **Semantic Ill-Formedness**

   ■ Cause and Effect (a claim that something outside a person is causing her to have an emotional response)

   ■ Mind Reading (a claim that one knows what another is thinking or feeling)

   ■ Presuppositions (assumptions that are implied in the speaker's language)

How to do it:

To learn to use the Meta Model, you need to be able to hear the distinctions and respond with an appropriate Meta Model question.

Learn the meta- model distinctions

The meta-model is a set of linguistic distinctions that allows you to understand a speaker's experience and get more precise information about the person's "map or model" of the world.

The distinctions fall into 3 sets

Gather information
Recognizing limits of the speaker's map or model
Recognizing semantic gaps

Listen for cues

These are linguistic cues for each distinction to which the attentive listener will be aware.

Ask appropriate meta model questions

For each linguistic cue, there is a specific question that allows you to gather informaiton, challenge limitations, or fill in the gaps in the speaker's presentation.

Maintain Rapport

Meta-model questions probe into another person's world. Be sure to maintain rapport and use good judgement about the use of these tools!

SIMPLE DELETION

With simple deletions, the subject and /or object of the sentence is missing or unclear. To recover it, ask, "Who or what, specifically?"

Sample: "I'm happy"

Meta Model Response: "About what, specifically?"

UNSPECIFIED "WHO" (REFERENTIAL INDEX)

In this instance, words and phrases in the speaker's language do not identify who is being referred to. If the word or phrase fails to identify a specific person or thing, the listener has identified a generalization.

Meta Model inquiry: "Who, specifically?" or "What, specifically?" or "Which _____, specifically?"

Sample: "They said to contact you."

Meta Model Response: "Who, specifically, said to contact me.?"

COMPARATIVE DELETIONS

Comparative deletions occur when an implied comparison is being made in the speaker's mind, but it is not clear what is being compared to what. Some of the key words to listen for include "enough," "too," "better," "best," and "most." The Meta Model response is "As compared to what (or whom)?"

Sample: "This computer is too expensive."

Meta Model Response: "It's too expensive compared to what?"

NOMINALIZATIONS

Nominalizations occur when an active process is changed into a static thing. The purpose of recognizing nominalizations is to assist the speaker in reconnecting his linguistic model with the ongoing processes in his experience. When nominalizations are used, static images are created in the mind of the listener and speaker. The use of the Meta Model in this case turns the static images into moving pictures, which provides a lot more information at the conscious level. You can turn a static image into a mental movie by changing the nominalized word to an active word using an "ing" form. For example, change "relationship" to "relating," "information" to "informing," and so on. When something can't easily be turned into an "ing" word, you can ask, "How, specifically?"

Sample: *"Mary is awfully passive for being such a free-spirited person."*

Meta Model Response: *"How exactly, is Mary Passive?" "What do you mean by 'free spirited?"*

Sample: *"My confusion prevents me from moving ahead."*

Meta Model Response: *"What is confusing you, and how?"*

UNSPECIFIED VERBS

Unspecified verbs are those that lack the specificity needed to completely understand the exact or true meaning intended in the communication. (All verbs can be further specified.) The Meta Model inquiry is "How, specifically?"

Sample: *"My father scares me."*

Meta Model Response: *"Scares you how?"*

UNIVERSAL QUANTIFIERS

Universal quantifiers are absolutes in the linguistic world. These are phrases such as "never," "all," "every," "always," and "no one." They are words that over-generalize from a few experiences to a whole class of experience. One way to use the Meta Model with absolutes is to back track the absolute word but exaggerate it with your tone of voice: "ALL? Really?" Another way is to chunk down the generalization by asking "Who (or what) specifically?" You can also ask for a counter-example.

☞ **Examples:**

- "She never arrives anywhere on time!"

  (Response) "NEVER?" "It is your experience that she is never on time?" "For anything!?"

- "It is impossible to get anything done on time."

  (Response) "Has there ever been a time when you did get something done on time?"

☞ **The procedure can be outlined as follows:**

Step 1. Listen to the speaker's language, identifying universal quantifiers.

Step 2. Inquire about the universality of the generalization.

Sample: "She works all the time!"

Meta Model Response: "ALL the time? Like 24/7, even when sleeping?"

MODAL OPERATORS OF NECESSITY

Modal operators of necessity are statements identifying rules about or limits to a person's behavior. Examples of Modal Operators related to necessity are "should/shouldn't," "must/must not," and "have to." To inquire about these limits, ask, "What stops you?" or "What would happen if you did (didn't)?"

Asking "What stops you?" helps the person to think about what experience(s) she had where she created this generalization. Asking "What would happen if you did (didn't)?" gets the speaker to consider consequences. Avoid asking "Why?" It sometimes might work to unearth high-quality information but more often will get defensiveness, explanations, or justifications.

☞ **Examples:**

- "I need to be more confident."
  (Response) "What stops you?"

- "I shouldn't tell them how I feel about that."
  (Response) "What would happen if you did?"

Sample: "Our new project must be completed by year's end!"

Meta Model Response: "Please tell me, what would happen if it isn't completed?"

MODAL OPERATORS OF IMPOSSIBILITY

Modal operators of impossibility are statements that describe what is considered impossible in the speaker's map of the world. They are identified by words such as "can't," "impossible," "not possible," and so on. Many people limit their world unnecessarily by thinking something difficult or unfamiliar is "impossible." It is often useful to challenge this limited thinking by asking: "What stops you?" or "What would happen if you could?"

Notice how these questions are typically more useful than asking "Why?" which often leads to rationalizations, defensiveness or explanations.

Sample: *"I can't apply for the promotion."*

Meta Model Response: *"What is stopping you from applying?"*

LOST PERFORMATIVES

Judgements are generalizations about right/wrong; good/bad, moral/immoral, etc. They are identified by words such as "best," "good," "bad," "stupid," "annoying," "right," "wrong," "true," "false," and so on. Although they have the weight of moral imperatives, they are still generalizations based on the speaker's own map of the world. A judgement requires three performatives: the judge, a thing being judged, and a standard on which it is judged. "Lost performatives" are the missing elements in a judgement.

For instance, if someone says, "it's bad to chew gum," they have provided only the thing being judged: chewing gum. But they have not provided the judge (according to whom?) or the standard (why is... or how is chewing gum bad? What is bad about chewing gum? How do you know?) You can also inquire about the consequences—what would happen if you chew gum? Three different people might say it is bad to chew gum. When asked, one might say "It rots the teeth according to the American Dental Association." Another might say, "I hate it when people throw gum down and it sticks to my shoe." A third might say, "Grandma said it is ill-mannered and not suited to polite society."

The mental strategy for using the Meta Model inquiry with Lost Performatives can be described as follows:

Step 1: Listen to the speaker's language for judgements about the world—these are identified with words in the same class as stupid, annoying, right, wrong, true, false, and so on.

Step 2: Note that this is a generalization about the speaker's model of the world.

Step 3: Since this is a generalization about the model and not about the world, the coach (effective communicator) may help the speaker to develop more possibilities within his model by uncovering the "lost performatives" in the judgement.

Sample: "*It's bad to be late.*"

(Response) "*Bad for whom?*" How is being late bad? What exactly is being late?

Sample: "*This is the right way to behave.*"

(Response) "*This is the right way for whom to behave?*" (*Notice that his clarifies the standard but does not specify the judge); According to whom? What behavior, specifically?*

CAUSE AND EFFECT

A Cause and Effect statement is made when a person attributes an internal state, such as a feeling, or a behavior to an external event or person when the connection is not clear. If someone says, "He made me do it," it is not clear what the person did that the speaker believed "caused" him to act. The Meta Model inquiry is, "How does X cause Y?"

Sample: "*This music annoys me.*"

(Response) "*How exactly does this music cause you to be annoyed?*"

Sample: "*He makes me mad.*"

(Response) "*How does his behavior make you mad?*"

MIND READING

Mind reading happens when a person claims to know what another individual is thinking or what is motivating the other person without any specific communication from the speaker about what is in his mind.

The Meta Model inquiry for this pattern is, "How do you know X?" This provides a way for the speaker to become aware of and even to question those assumptions that she may have taken for granted.

☞ **Examples:**

Sample: "*My dad doesn't care what I do.*"

(Response) "*How do you know that your dad doesn't care?*"

Sample: "*You're not going to like this, but ...*"

(Response) "*How do you know that?*"

Sample: "*I know you will think that this is a stupid question, but ...*"
(Response) "*How do you know that I'll think that it is stupid?*"

PRESUPPOSITIONS (SILENT OR HIDDEN ASSUMPTIONS)

What is it?

Presuppositions are (sometimes unconscious) assumptions that a person makes.

Why Use it?

In identifying presuppositions, the goal is to help the speaker identify those basic assumptions that narrow her model of the world and limit behavioral possibilities. Linguistically, these basic assumptions show up as presuppositions of the person's language. For example, to make sense out of the sentence, "I'm afraid that the new manager is as untrustworthy as the last one," you have to accept as true the idea that the original manager was untrustworthy.

How to use this information:

To identify presuppositions, ask yourself, "What must be true or assumed for the person saying this?"

The Meta Model response unmasks the silent assumption by asking for evidence or by back tracking the hidden assumption. Consider this statement: "If my boss knew how overburdened I am, he wouldn't keep dumping more responsibility on me." This sentence assumes that the person is overburdened, that her boss is giving her responsibility as a way to rid himself of them, that her boss is unaware of how she is overburdened, and that her boss's behavior would change if he knew about her feelings. Possible questions include the following: "How do you get yourself overburdened?" or "How do you know that your boss is unaware of this?" or "How do you know that he is dumping on you rather than entrusting you with responsibility?"

Sample: *"Since Monty is so mean, let's avoid him."*

What within the sentence must be true? Monty is mean; he should be avoided.

Meta Model Response: *"How is Monty mean?" "What will avoiding him get for us?"*

There are several types of key presuppositions:

- **Time**- This category presupposes that something will occur, and it is just a matter of when. Some of the time presuppositions are "when," "before," "since," "after," "next week," and so on.

  The sentence "Do you want to sign the contract before we have lunch?" presupposes that the contract will be signed.

  The sentence "Since we are meeting today, we can finish off the X project" presupposes that we are meeting and that we can finish the project.

- **Or/ordinal**- These presuppositions provide for a choice between options. Ordinal presuppositions put something into a sequence:

  The sentence "Shall we meet at your office or mine?" presupposes that we are going to meet, it is only a matter of where.

  The sentence "Will this be the first time that you have identified your personal criteria for work that motivates you?" presupposes that you will set your criteria.

- **Adverbs and adjectives**- These words modify sentences and add a descriptor. Notice that any "ly" word can be used as a presupposition.

  "I'm wondering how quickly you can identify the goals for your project." This sentence assumes that you will set your goals and the only question is the speed of your completion.

  "Fortunately, the whole team will be present, so all the questions can be answered." The assumption is that questions will be answered.

- **Awareness**- These presuppositions assume that something is the case and the only question is whether or not you are aware of it.

Awareness presuppositions include "aware," "realize," "recognize," "know," "see," "caught on," and so on.

"Are you aware of how often you already use these forms of language?" This sentence assumes that you use presuppositions, and it directs your attention to whether or not you are aware of this fact.

"It won't take our clients long to figure out that we provide the most timely service." This sentence presupposes that we provide the "most timely" service. The listener's attention is directed to the client's realizing the fact.

CRAFT OF COACHING

The coaching "crafts" below are a set of specific skills that can be used in coaching sessions. These are the "nuts and bolts" of coaching and are especially useful for coaching employees. The coach can easily incorporate many of these patterns into the coaching process at appropriate times. We offer an exercise for each of the coaching crafts that we use in coach training courses. The exercises require working with others or in small groups and we encourage you to find colleagues or friends with whom you can practice.

ACKNOWLEDGING

What is it?

Acknowledging is an act of recognizing positive behaviors, capabilities, beliefs, values, and personal traits as well as the personal struggles and challenges and how the client faces them. For example, the coach might say, "I know that you must be disappointed about not receiving the promotion—you definitely worked hard and were well prepared for it." It is "seeing" the client.

Why use it?

Often what's really going on with a person is not acknowledged. When the coach articulates it, then it becomes part of the conversation. It is different from praising. Praising is making a judgment or an evaluation of a person; acknowledging is about stating what is.

What does it do?

It creates a deeper rapport with the client.

ACKNOWLEDGING EXERCISE

Identify five people that you know or admire. Write an acknowledgment of who they are or what they have done to get to where they are today. Do the same with yourself: write an acknowledgement describing who you are or what you have done to become the person that you are now? Take a few moments and make a list of your accomplishments.

CHALLENGING

What is it?

Challenging is suggesting that your client do something that would take him well beyond his comfort zone. It must be a strong enough challenge that your client will actually resist it. For example, if you have a workaholic client whose life is way out of balance, you might challenge him to take two hours a day for pure personal fun and recreation. He may say that there's no way that can happen and give you a lot of reasons. You now have a place to begin negotiating for something that will move him toward what he really wants. If he is in conflict, this step will typically identify both sides of the issue, which you can then help him integrate or resolve the conflict.

Why use it?

Challenging is helpful in two ways. The first is that it gets your client to stretch beyond where she would go on her own. They say that life winners stretch themselves ten percent beyond their comfort zone. The second way that challenging is helpful is that it demonstrates that you believe in your client and that she has what it takes to move beyond where she thought she could go.

What does it do?

It motivates the client to go beyond where he would normally go on his own. An effective challenge gets push back on degree: the person refuses the challenge as given and offers a lesser stretch, which is still beyond what he might normally do.

CHALLENGING EXERCISE

Get together with two colleagues or friends. Each one lists three areas of personal or work life that are out of balance in some way. In turns, each one serves as a client, describing these imbalances and the other two serve as coaches working together to devise a challenge that would stretch the client well beyond her comfort zone. The client then works with the coaches to negotiate a counter-offer.

INTRUDING

What is Intruding?

Intruding is a way of politely interrupting your client so that she doesn't go on and on in some way that is not useful during the coach session. While coaching, you might intrude by doing the following:

- Backtrack your understanding of the story so far by providing a summary limited to the salient points. This can be followed by a question to refocus the client. For example, the client might launch into a story about a co-worker's attitude when the focus of the session is on "moving ahead on a project". You might simply say. "So this person can be difficult and you really want to move ahead with the project. Given that, what might you do to move it along?"

- Tell him that you are going to interrupt him. "I need to interrupt you for a moment." You can also make interrupting a part of the coaching agreement by discussing this in advance so that you have permission from the client to interrupt when you think it is necessary.

- Use a "relevancy Challenge:" Ask the client how the story is relevant to the agreed focus of the session. Or say: "Excuse me, I'm not certain where we are going with this."

- Use Meta Model questions such as "How specifically?" or "Where specifically?" or "Tell me what you mean by that."

- Redirect the conversation toward a more useful topic by asking something like "What did you learn from that?" or "What did having this experience mean to you?"

- Identify a positive intention for the long story: "I know you're going somewhere important with this story; what is it that you are really wanting now?"

Why use it?

Intruding as a useful skill for making the best use of coach time.

INTRUDING EXERCISE

In pairs as client and coach: The client tells a long rambling story, something she can go on and on about. As the client is telling the story, a coach's job is to interrupt the client and help to change the course of the story by trying out different coach skills, such as backtracking and redirecting to a pertinent topic; challenging relevancy of the story, asking the client to summarize: "What does that mean to you?" etc.

INQUIRY

What is it?

Milton Erickson, considered one of the world's foremost hypnotherapists and one of the early models for NLP, kept a number of objects in his office: small ornaments, unusual pencils, little figurines, and so on. At the end of a therapeutic session, Milton would often hand his client an object, telling the client that there is something with deep meaning for him in the object and that he should concentrate on it between their sessions. The client would often find that something important bubbled up from his unconscious mind through this experience. As a coaching skill, inquiry taps into this idea.

Why use it?

Inquiry is a powerful way for the client to maintain a conscious focus of attention on a new way of being in the world.

What does it do?

Inquiry is a question for reflection and self-discovery. With your inquiry, you offer a question to a client for her to ponder until you meet again. It is not necessarily a question that has a "right" answer.

Inquiry questions could include the following:

- What state of mind am I in, when I'm doing my best?
- What am I postponing?

- What am I holding back?
- What do I say "yes" to, and what do I say "no" to?
- What am I settling for?
- What do I really want here and now?

The book *Coactive Coaching* has a long list of inquiry questions. Some coaches maintain lists of inquiry questions from which they can choose.

INQUIRY EXERCISE

In a small group, brainstorm several useful inquiry questions for the following coach contexts: motivation, follow through, identifying what's working in your life, and getting past stuck places.

REQUESTING

What is it?

You can make a request of your client. Of course, you will only request what is relevant to your client's agenda. You might, for example, request that your client take action on something that he's been procrastinating about. You might also turn a client's complaint into an opportunity by suggesting that he consider making a request of someone else.

Why use it?

Requesting is used to nudge the client forward. For example, a client wants to change her own pattern of "complaining." You could request that the client practice identifying the hidden desire in each "complaint" that she brings to coaching. Notice how this re-empowers the client and keeps her from getting stuck in "victim mode."

Coaching is a process of asking high quality questions that move the client toward desired goals. This commonly involves requests to complete some assignment, follow through on something, or try out something new. When making a request, it is important for you as the coach to remain unattached to your idea. Even if you're pretty clear that your idea would be very helpful, the client has three choices when responding to a request: he can say yes, he can say no, or he can come up with a different possibility. If he says yes, employ the coaching craft of accountability. If he says no, you can ask him what he will do or how he wants to approach dealing with his issue. If he makes a counter-offer, you can again employ accountability: "Would you like to be held accountable for this?"

REQUESTING EXERCISE

Form groups of two and list five areas of life in which you have a complaint. The "client" presents each complaint in turn and the "coach" devises a request that could addresses the complaint. The coach offers each request, and the client can say "yes" or "no" or make a counter-offer.

CONTENT REFRAMING

Reframing is putting something into a different framework or context than it has been previously perceived. It helps to expand the client's possibilities. For example, imagine that a friend of yours walks by in the morning and does not respond to your friendly "hello." There are many meanings that you could take from this, and they will depend on your experience, your beliefs, and your mood. You might think that she simply didn't hear you, or that she doesn't like you, or that she's angry, or that she's rude, and so on.

Most clients spend much of their time thinking within the mental boxes that they have constructed in their lives. When clients display limited thinking, reframing offers new possibilities for understanding a situation in a broader way.

You can use the following exercise to reframe a problem and bring a new perspective to it:

Think of something that is annoying, that causes you concern (your child got a "D" on a test, your boss seems grumpy, and so on). Then ask your client (or yourself):

- How important will this be in ten years?
- In relation to all of the things the person does and all of their actions, behaviors, and traits, how important is this?
- How does this actually impact one's life?
- Name five things that this situation could mean that would not cause you the same concern.
- Reverse the limiting presuppositions. Ask: "How is the opposite of what you thought actually true?"

One-phrase Reframing

- Inspired by Robert Dilts, One-Phrase Reframing reframes pejorative statements about oneself or about others. The purpose is to help clients move past self-sabotaging limits by rephrasing the key words or statements that they make when describing their limitations.

For example: Notice how the following words get less pejorative, but could mean the same thing:

- cheap – frugal - thrifty
- compromising – considerate - respectful
- stuck in his head – mental – intelligent - brilliant
- selfish – aware of his own needs – looks after himself

Applying One-phrase Reframes

Change a word that has a limiting or negative connotation to a new word or phrase that is more positive or gives a wider perspective. Have the client finish the statement: "I stop myself because I _____." The client may say something like the following:

- I stop myself because I don't want to be criticized by someone.
- I stop myself because I am afraid I'll fail.
- I stop myself because I'll look foolish.
- I stop myself because I feel awkward about meeting new people.

Reframe using a new word with a more positive meaning or a wider context (time, people, or space). For example, you can change "look foolish" to "take a risk."

Client: "I stop myself because I am afraid I'll fail."

Possible Coach reframe: "It is good to calculate risks so that you can identify the resources you need to meet this challenge."

Client: "I stop myself because I am afraid I'll look foolish."

Possible Coach reframe: "It can be helpful to be sensitive about how you come across to others."

Client: "I stop myself because I am afraid I'll get criticized."

Possible Coach reframe: "Being prepared for feedback helps you to find the usefulness in it."

Client: "I stop myself because I am afraid I feel awkward meeting new people."

Possible Coach reframe: "It's good to be clear about your present state so that you can move beyond it."

Coach Session Overview

1. **Pre-Session**	• Preparing for the session • Make space for the client • Set intent for the session • Prepare your state (curiosity, not knowing, respect for the client, NLP presuppositions)
2. **Rapport**	• Creating Trust • Ease with the client • Noticing when rapport is breaking down and correcting
3. **Directionalizing**	• Open questions that you tailor for the person • Consquences of different openings
4. **Holding the space** (and agenda for the client)	• Maintaining the focus • Listening and backtracking • Getting specific • Listening beyond content – attending to process
5. **What's called for?**	• Coach flexibility • Fostering flexibility in the client
6. **Planning and Action**	• Movement • Decisions • Identifable steps • Evaluation of the plan
7. **C losure/ Follow -up**	• Backtrack of the session • Review Accountability/inquiry/assignment • Bridge to next meeting (date and time) • After session notes — issues, metaphors, "short hand"

COACH SESSION OVERVIEW

Each coaching session is a process in itself and the coach can use the "Coach Session Overview" to manage the steps within a coaching session. It covers everything from the pre-session preparation to post-session notes and follow-up. The coach can use this map to keep on track with the client in each session.

GAINING RAPPORT

Rapport can be defined as being "in sync" or "on the same wavelength" or "in harmony" with another person. It implies clear understanding and mutual credibility between two or more people.

The ingredients in rapport were an early discovery from modeling through NLP. Mirroring or matching certain aspects of a client's behavior creates natural rapport. These include posture, breathing, tone and tempo and volume of speech, and the process words. When rapport is achieved, mirroring is mutual.

Why use it?

When natural rapport occurs, the speaker and listener are "in sync," the communication flows smoothly, and both parties easily understand each other. In the coaching relationship, rapport makes communication between the client and the coach easier and provides the coach with a deeper understanding of the client's ongoing experience. It is the foundation for building trust, a key ingredient in all successful coaching

What does it do?

Have you ever seen geese flying south in formation through the winter with their movements synchronized or a deer carefully following their leader at the side of a mountain? All animals strive for synchrony in their world and research shows that human beings strive for synchrony as well. Even before birth, babies will move rhythmically to the tempo of their mothers' voices and will quickly adapt to the cadence of other voices they hear. This synchrony appears to be an innate human trait and forms a foundation for rapport.

Early in the field of NLP, it was noted that highly effective therapists, sales people, negotiators and other professional communicators quickly built high-trust relationships by matching the other person's behavior and experience. The degree to which you match or pace the behaviors of others is the degree to which you get into rapport with them. There are a number of behaviors that gifted coaches tend to match systematically. These include posture and gestures, voice tone, tempo and volume, the words used to describe sensory experience, and the rate of breath.

All of us tend to match the behavior of others with whom we're in rapport to some degree. By bringing this phenomenon into conscious awareness and actively pacing the behaviors and experience of others, you can gain rapport even with those with whom you have had difficulty in the past or those who tend to be very different from you.

How do I do it?

One of the easiest ways to gain rapport is to mirror posture. In our experience, it is comfortable and natural for most people to be mirrored. There's a Norman Rockwell illustration of a couple of New England women leaning over a picket fence, obviously sharing some very juicy information with each other. Each is a mirror image of the other. Paul McCartney plays guitar left handed. He once commented that he and right-handed John Lennon sat "mirroring" each other when they composed many of their songs and he believed this is one reason they were so prolific.

Matching another person's behavior as if you are looking at them in a mirror is called "mirroring." For example, if their left leg is crossed, you cross your right leg in the same position. If their head is leaning to their left, lean yours to the right. Matching or mirroring a person's posture and gestures over time is called "pacing." The goal of matching or mirroring behavior is to create rapport and to deepen your understanding of another's experience and not to mimic the other person. You want to generally emulate another's posture and gestures, not play "monkey see, monkey do." If you match or mirror movement for movement, many people will become consciously aware of it and may become uncomfortable or may even be offended. So, mirror with subtlety.

Be aware of your setting. Your office or work area may be set up in such a way as to make achieving rapport difficult and will limit your flexibility. Once we visited a bank president about some possible communication training, and we were seated in some very low, soft chairs. The bank president was perched behind his huge desk in a very high, oversized office chair, looking vulture-like down on us. Needless to say, the interview was made much more difficult for both the banker and ourselves until we could dislodge him to another setting.

Be aware of your own behavior and avoid getting into postures that preclude the other person's ability to mirror you. For example, if you're a man wearing slacks and you have your legs crossed, ankle resting on the knee, it would be very difficult for women in a skirt to match you. If you're communicating with a child or someone who's noticeably taller or shorter than you are, sit down to minimize the disparity. We once watched tall, Virginia Satir, the therapeutic genius who developed family therapy and who served as an early model for NLP, skillfully maneuver a short woman during a conversation in such a way that Virginia was able to step down two stairs to gain eye level.

You can determine whether you've achieved rapport by first mirroring your client's posture, and then shifting your own posture to "lead" the other person. If they shift with you, you have rapport. If not, go back to mirroring.

Pacing another person's posture and gestures is one set of behavior. Another set is to pace the tone, tempo, and volume of speech. Matching speech requires that you listen carefully at multiple levels. We do not match what the person is saying, but instead how they are saying it. Voice tones have a tendency to be high or low, loud or soft. Tempos can be fast or slow, with pauses or without pauses. This means that you have to listen to both content of words and to the form in which the person speaks.

Have you ever spoken to someone who speaks at a much slower tempo of speech than you? What is your likely response? For most of us, our tendency in this situation would be to speed up, finish their sentences and make gestures for them to move on in an attempt to get them to talk faster. On the other hand, have you ever talked to someone who speaks at a much faster rate than you? Typically, the experience of both parties is discomfort and confusion, often including negative judgements of each other: the slow talker judged as "stupid" and the fast talker judged as a "con."

Listen carefully to the other person, and then begin to alter your tempo of speech to match that of the other person. If their tempo is very different from yours, then move in gradual increments so that the change is not so obvious. A good strategy for building the skill of matching others voice tone tempo and volume is to begin practicing with the radio and TV. Some commentators are exquisite at matching others, and you might want to begin by observing these highly effective communicators on the radio in particular and notice how well they're matching the tone, tempo, and volume of the person calling in to gain rapport. Matching in the way that we've been suggesting is an excellent way to gain rapport over the telephone because the only behavior to match is the voice on the other end of the phone. Matching rate of speech is one of the single most effective strategies for call center personnel to increase caller comfort and responsiveness.

To practice, try matching during normal conversations. Listen to the tone and tempo of the other person. When you respond to their comments, do so by matching their tone and tempo. After practicing this continuously for a week or two, you will notice that matching becomes automatic for you and you will no longer have to think about it.

As we mentioned earlier, newborns will strive for synchrony by moving rhythmically to their mothers' voices. As a child grows and learns the ways of his or her language, culture, the family and peer systems in which he finds himself, the child learns to make sense of the world through the five senses. Human beings never experience the world directly. We experience the world as we represented it visually (mental pictures), auditorily (sounds and words), and kinesthetically (body sensations, internal and external feelings, plus motion). Smell and taste are generally less developed in Western culture, but also play a role.

☞ **Try these experiments and notice how they impact your level of rapport:**

1. Notice the person's posture, how he holds his feet, the angle of his head, and where he has his hands. Mirror this posture. Convincer: Try having a conversation where you first mismatch the other person's posture. Then match it. Notice the difference.

2. Match the rhythm and speed of another person's breathing. Convincer: Try having a conversation where you first mismatch the other person's breathing. Then match it. Notice the difference.

3. Match the tempo and tonality of the other person's speech. Convincer: Try having a conversation where you first mismatch the other person's voice. Then match it. Notice the difference.

4. Match the process words used (predicates that identify which of the sensory modes a person is thinking in: visual, auditory, or kinesthetic). Through the process words, or "predicates," people consistently report how they are thinking. It takes a little listening practice to identify these words, but it is definitely worth the effort.

People report which representation system they're using at any given time in their words. These words are called "predicates, verbs, adverbs, adjectives or process words." For example, if someone is most aware of the pictures they are making in a particular moment, they will use words such as "look, see, view, image, picture, bright, fuzzy, perspective," and so on. If they're most aware of sounds or words, you'll hear them use words like "say, tell, sounds, hear, click, buzz, discuss, explain," and other words describing sounds or words of speech. Those most aware of kinesthetic experience will use words like "feel, touch, grasp," words having to do with temperature such as "hot, cool, lukewarm," motion words like "jump, hop, push," and texture words like "rough, smooth, hard."

Sensory predicates reflect exactly how the person is thinking. When you hear phrases like "I just can't bring this idea into focus," people are literally making an internal picture that is not focused. When you hear a comment such as "Fred is a bright guy," the internal representation of Fred will be a bright picture. Matching the predicates or process words another person uses is a powerful way to gain rapport. In fact, if you're not pacing the other person's language, you are not matching their reality and their understanding of the subject at hand. They will then have to translate your words to make understanding of what you're saying.

Common Visual Predicates:

- **See**- "I see what you mean"
- **Picture**- "I can't picture that"
- **Perspective**- "Get a new perspective"
- **Blank**- "I just went blank"

- **Look**- "Look at this!"
- **Image**- "I need a clearer image of the problem"
- **Colorful**- "A colorful example is ..."

Common Auditory Predicates:

- **Rings a bell**- "This rings a bell!"
- **Static**- "She gives me a lot of static"
- **Tone**- "I don't like the tone of this"
- **Say**- "I'm only going to say this once"
- **Listen**- "Listen ..."
- **Clicked**- "Things just clicked for me"
- **Tells**- "Something tells me I should ..."

Common Kinesthetic Predicates:

- **Feel**- "I really feel good about this"
- **Touch**- "Get in touch with me"
- **Cold**- "He's cold and insensitive"
- **Walk**- "Walk me through this problem"
- **Get a handle**- "I can't get a handle on this"
- **Reach**- "I keep reaching for a decision"
- **Solid**- "Let's get a solid understanding of this"

Relatively early in life, most of us learn to favor one system over another. One child is more aware of visual experience, another more aware of sounds and words, and yet another, more aware of the way things feel in internal sensations. We think using all five senses all the time, and there is no "primary sense," but we tend to be more consciously aware of one system over others depending on the context we are in. Moreover, each of us is a human system. Every thought affects your body and your body experience affects your thoughts. The consistent favoring of one system over another becomes *habitual* over time. In other words, thought affects your body posture, your breathing, your patterns of movement, the tone and tempo of your voice, and the words you use to describe your experience.

A person who most often represents their experience kinesthetically will tend to have more rounded, sloping, relaxed shoulders. They may be more muscular or pear-shaped. They will have a slower and lower voice tone and will breathe lower in the abdomen. A person who is more aware visually will tend to have a more erect posture, quicker movements, more tension in the shoulders, a voice tone that is higher with a faster tempo and shallower breathing that tends to be higher in the chest.

Those most aware of words or who interpret their experience through verbal description are likely to stand with their shoulders back, head shifted back, with the chin higher and speak in a more monotone voice, and they may speak in quotes. Some auditory thinkers are more aware of tonal qualities. These tonal thinkers tend to have voices that are rich or musical. Earl Nightingale is a good example of someone who has a rich and resonant auditory voice tone. Tonal thinkers often will tilt their heads to the left and look down as they're talking to you to avoid being distracted by what they see. They are better able to hear tones by avoiding eye contact in many cases.

Since breathing shifts when your attention shifts from one representation system to another, matching another person's rate of breathing may be the most powerful method for getting in rapport. Donald Moine and John Herd in "Modern Persuasion Strategies," a book describing NLP methods for sales, indicated that they video-recorded top performing sales people in action and discovered many of them were naturally matching their customers breathing without knowing it. When they pointed this out, the sales people denied it, but soon became convinced of its utility after viewing the videos. When you breathe at the same rate as another person, it produces an unconscious bond, and in fact, will force you through your own physiology into representing information in the same system as the other person; thereby, altering your voice tone and tempo and the words you choose to describe your experience.

To practice matching others breathing, note that it is easier to see the breathing of most people from slightly to the side as opposed to facing them directly. Watch the diaphragm area, the shoulders and the back just below the scapular. When someone is speaking, notice when they inhale. This is generally audible even on the telephone. As with the other behaviors we have identified to pace, after you've consciously matched breathing for a while, you'll begin to discover that you are beginning to match naturally without having to think about it as you interact.

People often are attracted to occupations where they can be more effective given their more developed conscious senses. For example, someone who is more consciously aware of visual phenomena and can make pictures easily may become an architect, engineer, mathematician or artist. Those more aware of sounds with a highly developed auditory sense may be attracted to languages and music using their ability to make refined distinctions in tone, tempo and timbre are useful. Kinesthetic thinkers may be attracted to dance or athletics.

In summary, rapport is the ability to get on someone else's wavelength and develop a harmonious relationship regardless of context. It's dependent on your ability to pace or mirror the other person's behavior and experience. The specific behaviors identified to pace include:

- The posture and gestures of the other person. Again, not mimicking the other person, but instead, emulating their posture.

- The tone, tempo and volume of voice of the person you're talking with. You will be misunderstood and distrusted in some way if your voice is radically different.

- Matching the breathing rate of the other person will create effective rapport, and again, maybe the most powerful way to get on another person's wavelength.

- Listening for and using the predicates or process words the other person is using will help assure that understanding will occur.

Most "failure to communicate" is not because people are bad or stupid, it is merely a mismatch of language patterns and lack of rapport. Rapport skills may be the single most effective skill to develop as a coach or, indeed, in life.

HOLDING THE CLIENT'S AGENDA

In today's world, it is difficult to stay focused on our goals because we are faced with a thousand distractions on a daily basis. Coaching helps us to stay on track. Holding the client's agenda is the primary job of a coach.

Purpose:

- To help keep the client focused
- To provide boundaries for the client

Method:

1. Work with the client to establish an agreed agenda. This may include two levels:

    a. The larger set of values, dreams, and goals for which the client wishes to use coaching and the agreed primary focus of coaching. These are usually identified in the intake session or re- contracting sessions.

    b. The specific agenda and targeted focus established for the current session.

2. There are many methods for holding the client's agenda:

    a. Stating the agenda and restating it at specific times

    b. Backtracking and relating topics to agenda items

    c. Asking powerful questions based on the client's agenda

    d. Intruding when the client goes off agenda

    e. Challenging relevancy when the client goes off agenda

    f. Pointing out conflicts in agenda items

DIRECTIONALIZING THE COMMUNICATION

What is it?

Directionalizing is using your words and language structure to direct the conversation in a purposeful way. This is a skill that can make a tremendous difference in the outcome of a coach session or meeting. The first few words that the coach utters will set a direction. If the coach asks, "How has it been going since our last coach conversation?" the client will likely give a vague answer or will offer a lot of information that may not be useful for the coach session. If the coach says, "What is our goal for today?" The client will give a specific answer, usually about the direction she wants to pursue, which is much more useful. Remember, however, that the content of the coach session is the client's agenda, not the coaches.

Why use it?

When you "directionalize," you use language to lead a person or group's experience and increase the likelihood of a successful coaching session. As is mentioned above, doing so helps avoid getting too much content or irrelevant content. With this coaching skill, you can direct the coach conversation in a useful way. For instance, you can use certain powerful language patterns of influence—statements, words, or phrases—that create an assumption in a sentence and guide the listener's attention in relevant ways:

DIRECTIONALIZING COMMUNICATION EXERCISE

Create groups of three: A, B, and C. Write out three sentences that you might make as a coach when opening a coach session, after you've said your initial greetings. With assistance from A and B, identify the following:

1. What is presupposed?
2. What is the internal response of the listener? What is assumed in his internal experience as a result of the statement? Do the statements lead your client to the kind of attention and awareness you would like?

3. Revise your "directionalizing" statement to direct the listener in the way that you want. You might need to play with different opening statements until you find some that you like and work well for your coaching.

   Imagine that a trainer opens a new employee orientation session with the statement "I hope that this session is not too boring for you." What is presupposed in the statement? Where does it direct the listener's attention? How might the trainer restate it so that it moves the session along in a positive way? Notice the difference when the trainer says, "By the end of this session, you will know five things that are essential for your success here."

IMPORTANT COACH IMPLICATIONS

A coach opens a coach session by saying, "Tell me how it's been going since our last session." Put yourself in the client's position. What is your internal process? To answer the question, you need to internally review the past, sort through a lot of information, and try to pick out the relevant pieces. It is a very vague request and likely it could easily start the coaching session off track. Useful possibilities for opening a Coaching session include the following statements:

- What is our agenda for today?
- Where are you now, and where do you want to be by the end of this session?
- What do you want to accomplish today?
- Before we discuss your goals for today, tell me how it went for you on last week's assignment.

Each of these opening statements will direct the coach conversation in a useful way. Always remember to get clear about your goal before you get started. Once you know your goal, it is fairly easy to lead the conversation in a productive way.

OUTCOMES

REQUIREMENTS FOR SUCCESS

People are more committed to goals they set for themselves and that arise out of their desires and interests. The process of creating well-formed outcomes comes directly from NLP and is especially useful for the coach because it provides specific questions that can help an employee to formulate powerful goals.

What is it?

This set of 13 questions represents the requirements necessary to ensure a well-formed outcome – in other words, an outcome that should be ecological and appropriate and that will be achieved if the questions are answered properly.

Why use it?

Most outcomes are not really well formed, and thus have less potential for success. By responding to each question, the client has a much better chance of success. When an outcome is clear and congruent (not in conflict with forces within the individual), the client will organize his/her unconscious processes to achieve it.

How do you use it?

Asking the following questions meets the requirements to help ensure success:

1. **What do you want?**

   Is the outcome:

   - Stated in the positive (what you do want, not what you don't want)?
   - Can you initiate it?
   - Do you have control over what happens?
   - Is it a large global outcome or is it of manageable chunk size? Break it down into smaller outcomes if necessary.

2. **How will you know when you've got it?** (evidence)

3. **Is the evidence described in sensory based terms?** (see, hear, feel, smell, taste)

4. **Where, When and With Whom Do You Want It?** (context)

5. **What are the positive and negative consequences of getting your outcome?**

6. **What resources do you need to get your outcome?** (Information, attitude, internal state, training, money; help or support from others, etc.)

7. **What are you already doing to begin to achieve your outcome?**

8. **What will achieving that outcome get for you?** (Determine the real benefit beyond just getting the specific outcome.)

9. **Is the first step to achieving your outcome specific and achievable?**

10. **Is there more than one way to get your outcome?**

11. **What time-frames are involved?**

12. **What stops you from having your outcome now?**

13. **Imagine stepping into the future and having your outcome fully. Look back and determine what steps were required to achieve the outcome now that you have it.** ("Backwards Planning")

META-OUTCOME
OR *THE OUTCOME OF THE OUTCOME*

What is it?

Most of the goals we set are really means to a greater end. Meta-outcome goes beyond an initial goal to identify the dream or desire that the initial goal serves.

Why use it?

- To find critical motivational patterns and get beyond poorly formed goals
- To resolve conflicts between parts of oneself or between people
- To lead you to the client's real criteria

- Identifies what really motivates you (or a client) toward a goal
- Uncovers critical values or criteria
- Identifies the interest in a negotiation
- Identifies the benefit behind a feature or an activity

When addressing meta-outcomes with an individual:

Start with a goal or outcome. This can be any goal, but it is especially useful when a goal does not meet the criteria for a "well-formed outcome." An example of a poorly formed outcome would be, "I want the customers to show me more respect."

Imagine the outcome is actually fulfilled and ask, "What would having this outcome fulfilled (customers treat you with respect) do for you?" You are asking for the outcome of the outcome. The client might say, "If customers treat me with more respect, I will feel confident handling their complaints."

Notice whether or not the answer is stated positively and is truly within the person's control. Does the answer include an inner state or a value? "Confidence" is an inner state.

If the answer is not stated positively or is outside the person's control, then repeat the meta-outcome question with the goal from the answer. For instance, the response, "The customers wouldn't be so abusive," is stated negatively and is outside of the person's control. You would repeat the meta-outcome question with the following question: "If the customers weren't so abusive, what would that do for you?" If the response is, "It would be easier to do my job," this is stated positively and may be within the person's control. It would be worthwhile to ask the meta-outcome question again to get to an inner state or value: "And if your job was truly easier as a consequence, what would that do for you?" "Then I would feel more confidence."

Repeat back the key words and phrases and confirm them with the client. "So, what you really want is to feel more confidence when dealing with your customers. Is that right?"

Using meta-outcome to resolve conflict between people:

Listen to the position advocated by each party and backtrack the positions to ensure understanding.

Ask each party what fulfillment of their position would do for them. The idea is to move beyond conflicting positions to higher-level motivation. Continue asking the meta-outcome question until you arrive at a shared outcome or at outcomes that are compatible.

Point out to the parties how they both want the same or similar goals, and then use this frame to gain cooperation and resolve the conflict.

☞ Questions to Determine Meta-Outcomes:

1. What will having that get (or do) for you?
2. How is that of value to you?
3. What is your goal in doing that?
4. What will that allow you to do, or to have, or to be?

☞ Steps to Determine Meta-Outcomes:

1. Set the context and state a position (outcome).

   Examples of positions:

   "I am going to starve myself to lose weight."

   "I can't apply for the job I want."

   "I need to be responsible for everything that happens in my office"

   "I want to be able to stay calm when my wife/husband yells at me."

2. Backtrack your understanding of the client's position and ask one of the meta-outcome questions.

META-OUTCOMES CASE STUDY

Jack, the manager of a new marketing campaign, had been out of the office for one week on company business. Before leaving, he found out there was some tension between Mike and Sandy, and he was surprised to find it had escalated to the point of threatening the functioning of the whole project team. He knew that he needed to act quickly to resolve the matter.

He brought Mike and Sandy together for a meeting to resolve the conflict. Jack started by taking the time to learn the positions of each party and then to ask each person some meta-outcome questions.

Mike felt that Sandy was taking short cuts and compromising quality. He wanted her to slow down, attend to the details more, and talk with him before she took certain actions. When asked what having Sandy behave this way would do for him, Mike said that it would ensure that the project was done right. Jack repeated the meta-outcome question, and Mike answered that having the project done right would make the company look good and that he would feel a sense of accomplishment. Going one step further, Mike said that this outcome would mean the project was a success and that he would be proud to have worked on it.

Sandy felt that Mike was holding everything up. She wanted Mike to "loosen up" and be more creative in addressing needs rather than doing everything by the book. Jack asked her what having Mike behave this way would do for her, and she replied that it would free her up to get things done without worrying about Mike's demands. Jack continued with meta-outcome questions, and Sandy reported that being freed up to get things done would mean that they could get the project done successfully and, ideally, ahead of schedule. And this would allow her and the project team to stand out in the company.

As they spoke about their meta-outcomes, Mike and Sandy both realized that they wanted the same general goal: a successful project outcome. They were also surprised to learn that they both wanted to be proud of the project. This point of agreement gave them inspiration to find a working compromise. Sandy agreed to talk with Mike ahead of time on specific matters, and Mike agreed to be open to alternative solutions as long as product quality was not compromised. The tensions that previously threatened the whole project were resolved in a single meeting of less than thirty minutes simply by asking meta-outcome questions!

STORYBOARDING YOUR FUTURE
BACKWARD PLANNING FOR LONG-TERM GOALS

What is it?

Storyboarding is a process of backward planning key steps toward accomplishing your goal and making dreams come true. This is a great tool for coaching employees because it teaches them how to make a road-map to achieving long term goals and maintaining their own motivation.

Why use it?

- To build a bridge between the current state and a long-term goal using backward planning

What does it do?

- Provides a link between current activities and long-term goals
- Identifies major milestones to mark progress toward long-term goals

How do I do it?

1. Create a well-formed outcome with a rich, full representation of a long-term desirable future. Determine an appropriate time frame for completion of the goal (six months, one year, three years, and so on).

2. Identify the halfway point between now and the desired future. For instance, if the goal were one year away, this "midpoint" would

be six months away. Identify what could be happening at the midpoint that would be clear and strong indicators of progress toward the desired goal. Using these indicators, create a representation of this halfway point, and place it in the appropriate spot between now and the desired future.

3. Now identify a halfway point between now and the midpoint just created in Step 2. This will be a "quarter point" on the way to the final goal. For instance, if the goal is one year, the midpoint is six months, and the quarter point is three months away. Identify what could be happening at the quarter point that would be clear and strong indicators of progress toward the midpoint and, hence, the goal. With these indicators, create a representation of this quarter-point landmark and place it in the appropriate spot between now and the midpoint.

4. Create a halfway point between now and the quarter point. This will be an "eighth point" on the way to the final goal. For instance, if the goal is one year, the midpoint is six months, the quarter point is three months, and the eighth point is six weeks away. Identify what could be happening at this eighth point that would be clear and strong indicators of progress toward the quarter point and, hence, the goal. Using these indicators, create a representation of this eighth-point milestone and place it in the appropriate spot between now and the quarter point.

5. Identify the next steps that are already underway or that can be taken immediately that move toward the "eighth point" outlined in Step 4.

6. Create a line that goes from the goal-setter (at "Now") through all of the above points and directly to the desired goal in order to create a strong and clear connection between all of these steps. Doing so will make the long-term goal an inevitable consequence of the steps along the way.

7. Test to find out how attainable the goal seems now with a storyboard that links all the appropriate stages to the desired goal.

Powerful Questions and Techniques for Coaches and Therapists

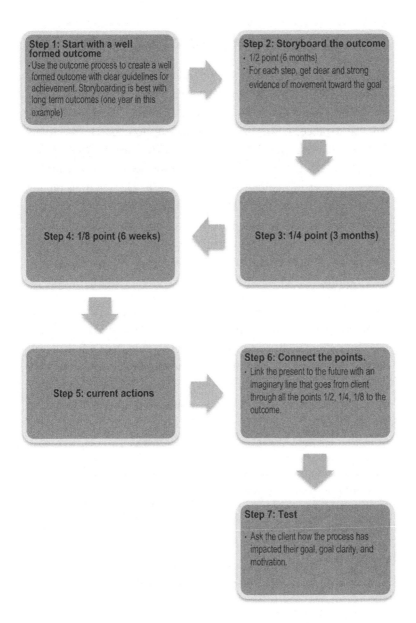

Step 1: Start with a well formed outcome
· Use the outcome process to create a well formed outcome with clear guidelines for achievement. Storyboarding is best with long term outcomes (one year in this example)

Step 2: Storyboard the outcome
· 1/2 point (6 months)
· For each step, get clear and strong evidence of movement toward the goal

Step 4: 1/8 point (6 weeks)

Step 3: 1/4 point (3 months)

Step 5: current actions

Step 6: Connect the points.
· Link the present to the future with an imaginary line that goes from client through all the points 1/2, 1/4, 1/8 to the outcome.

Step 7: Test
· Ask the client how the process has impacted their goal, goal clarity, and motivation.

STORYBOARDING CASE STUDY

Mark had studied diligently for several years to become a mediator. He wanted to start a mediation practice but felt overwhelmed and did not know where to start. Storyboarding his future seemed an excellent way to proceed. First, he defined the long-term goal by specifying the conditions and details of the outcome. Mark wanted to work four days per week, five hours per day, and provide at least seventy-five hours of direct mediation services per month. He was transitioning out of employment with the state of California and wanted to maintain an income. He also thought that he could use his experience to work with government employees but was not limiting himself to this population. He believed that he could accomplish this goal in eighteen months.

At the halfway point (nine months), he would have an established the mediation practice with a minimum of thirty client-contact hours per month or about eight hours per week. He would have a fully developed a Web site, have established a network of referral sources, have written at least two articles for publication in local papers, and be actively marketing his services. He would be getting referrals from satisfied clients. He would have reduced his state employment to part-time hours or about twenty-four hours per week.

At the quarter-way point of four and a half months (eighteen weeks), he would be providing ten hours mediation per month. He would have designed and published the Web site. He would have a network of potential referral sources, including attorneys and financial planners. He would have joined the local Chamber of Commerce and at least one other networking source. He would have reduced his work time with the state to thirty-two hours per week.

At the eighth point (nine weeks), he would have started marketing his mediation services and have at least two clients. He would have discussed his long-term plans with his manager at the state, whom he felt was supportive of his goals, and created a plan for reduced time.

Mark was already taking steps by completing his mediation training. He was working on identifying his strengths as a mediator and drafting a write-up of his philosophy of mediation for inclusion on his Web site. These topics became the focus of the immediate coaching activity. Moreover, he began conducting research on how to set up an account for accepting credit cards, and he had gotten support from his wife to begin setting up an office at home.

At the end of the storyboarding session, Mark felt that he had a clear plan of action and no longer felt overwhelmed. He felt renewed enthusiasm for his career choice and was eager to proceed.

STATE MANAGEMENT

What is it?

This is a process to be able to choose the state of mind that you want in any context. Many life challenges arise because people do not manage themselves well and act out of non-resourceful states. Coaching clients to manage their own state empowers them to get better results on the job and in life.

Why use it?

- To be able to access and maintain the state of mind that is most useful for a specific context—examples of states include being accepting, articulate, relaxed, focused, playful, and so on
- To increase flexibility and personal power
- To manage yourself and maintain a resourceful frame of mind

What does it do?

- Offers a powerful way of programming yourself now to automatically access the state when you want it
- Allows you to identify a desired state for a particular context

- Provides a method for accessing the desired state
- Provides a means to maintain the state for the appropriate time

How do I do it?

1. Describe the situation or context in which you want to access a certain state. Identify whether you want to succeed at a certain performance (for example, singing), to solve a problem (for example, working through a computer glitch), to deal with others (for example, resolving a problem with your boss), or to do a task (for example, writing a project plan). Identify who, what, where, and when. Consider the activities that go before and after the context.

2. Identify the state of mind that would be appropriate or most powerful in the situation: playful, alert, flexible, and so on. Consider the following:

   - What are your goals and intents for your state in the situation?

   - What evidence will let you know that you have accessed the desired state (breathing fully, smiling, staying focused, and so on)?

   - What will you do to achieve and maintain the state (technique, posture, mental set, intent, and so on)? Consider several ways that you can maintain the state.

   - What potential problems could arise that could throw you off in relation to your state? What will you do to regain it? Consider several ways to regain the state if you get thrown off.

Step 1: Specify the Context	Step 2: Identify the desired state	Step 3: Considerations in identifying a state
• Describe the situation or context in which you want to achieve a certain state such as: • Performing • Problem solving • Relating to others • Accomplishing a task	• What is an appropriate, powerful state that supports effectiveness in the situation?	• Goals and Intents: What is your goal in the situation? • Evidence: How would you know you are in the desired state? • Actions: What steps or actions can you take to initiate the state? • Recovery: What can you do to recover the state if you get thrown off?

STATE MANAGEMENT CASE STUDY 1

William was about to make a major sales presentation that could give him a hefty commission and add a significant contract to the company's book of business. He wanted to be at his best and chose this goal as the focus of a coaching session. State management seemed an appropriate coaching tool for William's situation.

William described the context as the conference room at the host company. He had been there once before for a preliminary meeting and had met two managers that would be involved in the decision. The meeting would include these two managers, the CFO, and the CEO of the company. This was clearly a "performance context." Before the meeting, William would organize his materials and make sure that the Power Point presentation and other materials were in place and ready to go. He had arranged with the managers to arrive ten minutes early to set up everything in the conference room. After the meeting, he hoped to be celebrating a signed contract.

William's goal was to "wow" them. He intended to be upbeat, professional, enthusiastic, and fully prepared to handle any question that might arise. He noted that he was at his best when he adopted an attitude of detachment from the goal of making a sale and instead focused on the people in the room and the moment. As evidence of this state, he imagined himself standing tall, feeling fluid in his body, and being mentally clear, focused, and upbeat.

When asked how he might achieve this state, William said that it helped to remember two things. First, he thought of his belief in his company and the product. Second, he thought of how he really likes people and that "high-level executives" are just people. When he focused on them as people, he felt connected to them, ready to hear what they had to say, and eager to make sure that they understood what he had to offer. He also felt less drive to "make the sale" and more confident that he could make the best presentation possible.

He felt that he could maintain the state by focusing on the process and the people, not on the end result. William came up with several methods to regain the confident state should he get thrown off, including a self-anchor for being present, use of his PowerPoint presentation as a process anchor, keeping his attention focused on the other people, and using the rapport that he developed previously with the managers.

William's confidence seemed to grow with each answer to the state management questions. At the end of the process, he was glowing and said that he felt sure he could do his best. At the next coaching session, William reported that the officers did not sign the contract at the end of the meeting as he had hoped, but the state management process worked beautifully, and he felt that he had done his best. He then announced that they had called two days later to negotiate the details and had signed the contract the next day!

STATE MANAGEMENT CASE STUDY 2

Fred was applying for a new position. Part of the application process included an interview with a panel of directors, and he was a bit nervous about this. Using the state management process above, Fred first thought through the context in detail. He identified the state that he wanted to be in during the interview. He wanted to be articulate, flexible, warm, and have a sense of conviction. He identified the physiological and mental evidences for each state. Then he decided how he would access the states.

He remembered times when he had been in each state. He mentally stepped back into the experience and relived it. He noticed his feelings and how his body felt during the experience. He noticed that if he stood up while doing this, it was easier to truly access the states.

He used appropriate language to help drive the states. For example, to access the state of conviction, he said, "I know that I know" in a convincing tone of voice. To elicit warmth, he imagined looking at each person on the panel and thinking, "I am glad you're here."

He found postures that supported each state and found ways to move his body to enhance the state congruently.

He then thought about what might happen that could throw him off balance: being asked tricky questions, rudeness on the part of a panel member, and so on. He then rehearsed dealing with strange questions or off-putting behavior until he was satisfied that he would maintain the state.

He later reported to his coach that the interview was a "breeze."

Techniques

APPRECIATIVE INQUIRY

Appreciative Inquiry (AI) is an approach to personal and organizational development based on social constructionist theory. It states that human systems are made and imagined by those who live and work within them. AI has grown rapidly since its inception in 1987 from the work of David L. Cooperider, PhD, and Suresh Srivastva, PhD, from the Weatherhead School of Management at Case Western University.

Traditional change management efforts are deficit based and focus on fixing what is wrong, an approach that presupposes that there is something wrong with the system. AI is strength based and places the focus squarely on what is right and what is working within a system. The goal is to find what you appreciate, inquire into it, dialogue about it, and build on the positive core within a person or organization.

AI is both a perspective and a set of practices. It has been applied to organizational change with major corporations, systemic changes in social systems or groups, and to individual change.

People are more successful and have happier lives when they build on their strengths. The model of AI provides a basic framework for effective coaching because it identifies and builds on strengths. The basic idea is simple: find what you appreciate (a strength) and inquire into it. The format for the inquiry is to go backward, inward, and then forward.

Why use it?

- To bring the best of the past forward
- To identify and build on strengths

What does it do?

- Provides resources useful for specific situations
- Provides a model for learning from experience
- Offers a basic format for effective questioning in the coaching context (backward-inward-forward)

How do I do it?

1. Identify something that you appreciate about yourself (an activity, a value, or a strength) or something that you appreciate in a system (a company activity, company values, or company strengths).

2. Go backward: Recall a time when the activity, value, or strength was expressed. This process will be much more effective when you (or your client) recalls and relives an actual experience.

3. Go inward: Inquire into the experience while the person relives it to identify the conditions and ingredients that made it work. Here are some questions to ask or areas to consider:

   a. Conditions

      - What were the conditions in the environment that allowed the strength to be expressed?
      - What did others or the system do that helped to express the strength?

   b. Ingredients

      - What state of mind goes along with the strength?
      - What was your goal?
      - What did you do to express the strength?
      - How did you do it?
      - What ingredients contributed to expression?

   c. Beliefs and Values

      - What beliefs and values help to express the strength?
      - What was your part in making it happen?

4. Go forward: Take what is learned from going "inward," and bring these gifts forward into the present and the future. You can apply what is learned to almost any situation, and it does not need to be only for those situations where the strength "naturally" occurs. In

fact, the conditions, ingredients, beliefs, values, and contributions provide much material that can be helpful (in surprising ways) in moving toward any goal or issue in a coaching context. Ask, "How can you use what you have learned here for (the goal or issue)?"

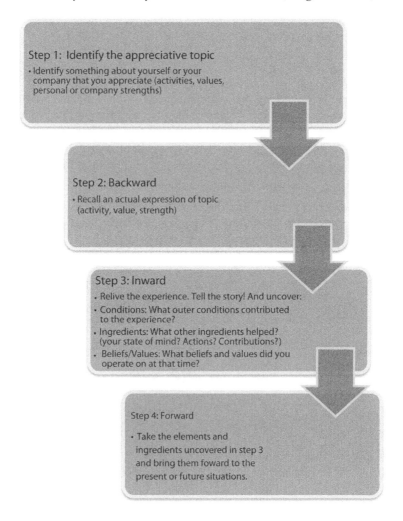

Step 1: Identify the appreciative topic
- Identify something about yourself or your company that you appreciate (activities, values, personal or company strengths)

Step 2: Backward
- Recall an actual expression of topic (activity, value, strength)

Step 3: Inward
- Relive the experience. Tell the story! And uncover:
- Conditions: What outer conditions contributed to the experience?
- Ingredients: What other ingredients helped? (your state of mind? Actions? Contributions?)
- Beliefs/Values: What beliefs and values did you operate on at that time?

Step 4: Forward
- Take the elements and ingredients uncovered in step 3 and bring them foward to the present or future situations.

APPRECIATIVE INQUIRY CASE STUDY

Julie was stuck on a project at work; she had to roll out an in-house training academy. The project required collaborative teamwork with members of another department who were less invested in the project, and she was falling behind schedule. There was a history of strained relations between the two departments from before her tenure, and she felt some people were holding old grudges against her. She wanted to resolve the matter herself rather than taking a complaint to her superiors.

Using AI, Julie recalled a time, several years earlier, when she had experienced incredible collaboration working with a trade association to coordinate a large vendor trade show. She had seen a high level of cooperation, even though association staff members held very different positions within the association and all had primary duties unrelated to the trade show project. Staff from affiliate member organizations also volunteered time to help with the project. She described the following ingredients and conditions in the collaborative effort:

- Shared excitement about the result
- Willingness to help each other out
- Creativity in handling barriers
- Clarity about what could or could not be done
- Permission to request time or activity from others (not only from upper management but from each other)
- Respect for each other's duties and time constraints

Julie's part in facilitating the collaboration was her own enthusiasm, which allowed her to communicate the vision of a sterling trade show that would make the members of the trade association proud. She recalled specifically that she would make requests of others with a two-fold goal: first, to get a task accomplished, and second, to get ideas and input from the person that could help her to move forward, especially if the person was unable or unwilling to help directly.

Julie recalled how she would get herself through the tough times by thinking about how amazing it would be if she pulled off a success despite the odds against her. After all, she had no staff, no real authority, and very few resources. She needed others to make projects happen, and they were already very busy with their own workloads.

Julie immediately realized that she had gotten caught up in the politics of the organization and had lost sight of the project vision. She had also avoided using her own manager because she feared that her concerns about the other department would be perceived as blame and would make a bad situation worse. Julie recognized direct parallels between the two situations and how she could use all that she had learned then to help her now.

Julie felt clear about what she needed to do. First, she needed to revitalize the vision of a superb training academy that would be a mark of distinction in the organization. She knew that she could formulate requests, incorporating the vision, in a way that would take some of the pressure off of others, making it easier to get them involved. She began feeling excited about "pulling it off" despite the history in the organization and about how this achievement could really improve her job, and her perspective, overall.

GREGORY BATESON'S PROBLEM-SOLVING STRATEGY
(ORIGINALLY DEVELOPED BY ROBERT DILTS)

What is it?

This technique, adapted by Robert Dilts from the work of Gregory Bateson, uses life experiences to solve problems or gain new perspective on difficult or challenging situations. It is unique in that the resources to solve a problem are obtained from a life experience that is totally unrelated to the challenge or difficulty. This new life experience is used to metaphorically frame the challenge and find creative solutions for the problem situation.

Why use it?

- To solve problems
- To obtain perspective on difficult or challenging situations
- To get out of or beyond "stuck states"

What does it do?

- Provides access to resources from the client's life experiences
- Uses metaphor to discover creative solutions to challenges

How do I do it?

This technique works best when you use "spatial anchoring." Spatial anchoring allows you to separate aspects or steps in the process by separating them in space. Create three physical locations in front of you and designate them as follows:

Problem Space		Resource Space
	Observer	

1. Think of some problem with which you are at an impasse, such as an "inability to concentrate on studies."

2. Step into the Problem State location; associate into the problem situation and experience what is happening.

3. Step out of the Problem State and into the Observer State Position.

4. Think of something that you do that is completely unrelated to the problem situation and is a resource for you—an activity or ability (such as skiing) that really gives you a sense of identity, mission, creativity, passion, and so on.

5. Step into the Resource State location and associate into the resource experience.

6. Look over at the Problem State from the Resource State. Make a metaphor for the problem situation in the context of the resource activity. That is, if the problem were being expressed in the context of the Resource State, what would be happening? (An inability to concentrate is like constantly getting one's skis crossed.)

7. Find the solution to the problem from within the metaphor. (When you are getting your skis crossed, it is best to slow down, focus on moving one ski, and let the other ski follow.)

8. Step out of the metaphoric situation into the Problem State and bring the solution with you. Translate and apply the metaphoric solution to the original context. (When it is time to study, slow down, pick one thing to study, focus on it, and let the other things follow.)

GREGORY BATESON'S PROBLEM-SOLVING STRATEGY
CASE STUDY

Larry had failed the bar exam on three separate occasions. He was scheduled to take the exam for the fourth time in a week. In his coaching session, he described how thoroughly he had studied and how well he had performed on the practice exams; he always scored well above passing level. But at test time, he would "lose it," become confused by the questions, and fail to finish in the allotted time.

Applying Bateson's Problem-Solving Strategy, Larry used his practice as a martial artist for a resource context. Considering the problem from this perspective, he realized that poor functioning in the test was like being too focused on yourself in sparring and not noticing your opponent. The solution in sparring was to focus on the opponent, trust your training, and let your responses come automatically. He understood that the key was having a kind of panoramic view of the situation. When he took this idea into the Problem State, he imagined letting himself have his attention directed outward in a more panoramic view, and he instantly felt the feelings that he had when sparring. He immediately felt more relaxed and more capable of responding to test questions. One week later, Larry passed his exam.

NEW BEHAVIOR GENERATOR

Why use it?

New Behavior Generator was developed from modeling the mental process-es that quick learners use to put new behaviors into their lives. It can also be used to create a new habit and immediately adopt it. Therefore, this is a great tool for coaching a client to create and implement new skills or behaviors. When done properly, the client will automatically remember to use the new behavior and should not have to consciously try to remember it.

What does it do?

This process uses mental imagery and rehearsal to quickly learn a new be-havior. It allows one to "program one's self now" to automatically remember to do the new behavior later.

Here is an example. A client found herself getting involved in her e-mail when she first arrived at her office. She realized that when she did this, she tended to respond to e-mail, which took up her time and was not in align-ment with her real priorities. Instead, she wanted a new habit of taking the time to plan her day in the morning before she did anything else. The New Behavior Generator helped her to install the new behavior in such a way that she remembered to do her planning first and felt motivated to continue to meet her top priorities.

How do I do it?

1. Find a "stuck" situation where you are not as resourceful as you would like to be. Review it as if it were a movie that you were watching with you in it. Notice how you typically behave in that situation.

2. Find a resource state that might work better for you than what you are currently doing in the stuck situation. If you can't find a resourceful behavior that you have used in the past, either pretend that you can (As If) or think of someone else who is resourceful and model them.

3. Review the stuck situation using the new behavior as if it were a movie that you were watching with you in it. If you like the way

that it looks, go on to Step 4. If you don't like the way it looks, then go back to Step 2 and find another resource that might work and test it again in Step 3.

4. Review the stuck situation using the new behavior as if you are actually experiencing it now. Jump into your body, into the movie, and experience it. If you like the way it feels, go on to Step 5. If you don't like the way it feels, then go back to Step 2, find another resource and then on to step 3, etc..

5. Mentally rehearse the new behavior in the appropriate future contexts: Think of an external cue that will remind you to automatically use the new behavior in the kind of context where you would have been stuck in the past. Imagine that external cue (hearing something or seeing something in your environment) and feel yourself using the new behavior in that situation. Do this step several times in several different contexts to anchor in the behavior and make it automatic.

NEW BEHAVIOR GENERATOR CASE STUDY

John had a hard time getting up in the morning. He would hear the alarm go off, but he would then push the snooze button, roll over, and go back to sleep. He continued to do this repeatedly until the last minute. He would then get up and rush around, often being late for meetings or arriving at work feeling frazzled.

He wanted to get up earlier and feel good about it, though he could not think of a time that he had ever done so as an adult. Since he did not have a past behavior to use, he thought of a friend who was "a real morning person" and who always arose easily. He asked her what she did. She was the kind of person who woke up early each morning, "leaping out of bed and ready to go."

In thinking it through, his friend realized that when she heard her alarm clock sound, she would say to herself, "It's time to get up." Then she would leap out of bed and stretch her arms. John thought this sounded like a good idea. Using the New Behavior Generator process, he ran a mental movie of sleeping in and pushing the snooze button repeatedly. Then he ran a movie of what he wanted to do instead. He saw himself lying in bed, hearing his alarm clock ring, and saying to himself, "It's time to get up." He then saw himself jump out of bed and stretch his arms. He liked the way that looked, so he tried it out as a rehearsal. He imagined being in that situation, hearing the alarm, and jumping up and stretching. His body said, "No way am I going to jump out of bed, first thing in the morning!" He then found a way to modify hearing the alarm and turning it off as he said, "Time to get up." Then he rehearsed slowly sitting up, getting up, and stretching. He felt that this would work much better for him. He rehearsed this process several times. He later reported that it worked beautifully: the very next morning he had gotten up and stretched the first time that the alarm went off.

RESOURCE STATES

What is it?

We all experience times when we get "stuck" or respond poorly to life situations. This process allows you to gain new perspective on situations that trigger ineffective reactions and provides you or your client with new choices and responses.

Why use it?

Resource states are widely applicable in lots of coaching situations and are especially useful for times when your client gets stuck (anxiety, anger, embarrassment, and so on) and is unable to respond appropriately and resourcefully.

What does it do?

This process is useful when the client identifies a situation in which being in a non-resourceful state prevents her from responding in a healthy and appropriate way. For the process to succeed, it is important to isolate the situational trigger that initiates the non-resourceful state (words, tone, non-verbal behavior, place, and so on). The idea is to help the client to detach from the situation, gather her resources, and then step back into the situation with more resources. If done properly, the situation will change dramatically for the client.

How do I do it?

1. Have the client identify an actual example of the triggering situation and mentally step into the situation at the point when she first realizes that she is having the undesired response.

2. Have the client dissociate from the situation by having her take a deep breath and step back to watch herself in that situation. To create a greater sense of detachment, have the client imagine that she is watching herself through a thick Plexiglas window.

3. Have her identify the most appropriate responses for the "you over there." Assist the client to build up a complete representation of this new response.

    Here are some ideas for building the new resource:

    - See the big picture from a distance such as the "Jolly Green Giant's" perspective).

    - If it is a still picture, then make a movie out of it.

    - Have the person freeze frame the mental movie of the situation and then step out of it. Access and feel the resources and then step back into the scene.

    - Consider the situation from the perspective of ten years from now.

    - If appropriate, add humor or make some element of the situation incongruous—for example, have the person watch the situation from a distance and change the sound to puppies barking; put music behind the scene; run the situation at half speed and the client at double speed, popping them out at the end before the situation is over.

    - Anchor a state of inner peace and witness the situation, then step into it.

4. Now have the client associate by stepping back into the situation with her new response. If a new response is needed or if adjustments need to be made in the selected response, repeat Steps 3, 4, and 5. Once a congruent and positive solution is achieved, have the

client repeat the entire process (Steps 1 to 5) as many times as is necessary to learn the strategy.

5. Bridge the new behavior into the real world by rehearsing Steps 1 to 5 with a future example.

6. Test by directing the client to think of a future or past example of that context and calibrate for response.

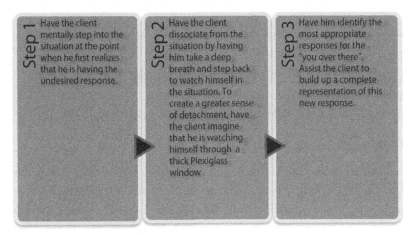

Step 1 Have the client mentally step into the situation at the point when he first realizes that he is having the undesired response.

Step 2 Have the client dissociate from the situation by having him take a deep breath and step back to watch himself in the situation. To create a greater sense of detachment, have the client imagine that he is watching himself through a thick Plexiglass window.

Step 3 Have him identify the most appropriate responses for the "you over there". Assist the client to build up a complete representation of this new response.

RESOURCE STATE CASE STUDY

Iris was dealing with a judgmental coworker and found herself avoiding this person, even though interfacing with him was necessary for her job. The issue was amplified the day she came for coaching reporting this coworker repeatedly criticized her report at a staff meeting earlier that day. She then mentally stepped back from the scene and went to an Observer position, watching herself at the meeting. This gave her the distance to add in new resources, which she did as described above. She tried out all of these new perspectives and reframes. (Note that you don't typically need to have the client do all of them; you might just select the one or ones that intuitively seem most likely to make the greatest change.) By the end, Iris literally could not get her angry feelings back after adding in these new resourceful ways of thinking. Notice that the goal here is to empower the client, not to try to change the other person. But Iris later reported a surprising result, and one that happens often in our experience: the coworker changed his behavior toward her and spontaneously stopped criticizing her. She clearly was giving him something different to respond to while she was taking a new perspective on the situation.

A CREATIVE SOLUTION-FINDING PROCESS: REFRAMING
REFRAMING AS A CONSCIOUS COACH PROCESS

What is it?

This process is designed to engage creative problem solving while respecting the ecology of the system. At some point, everyone faces the challenge of changing a limiting behavior: those things that we do but wished we didn't do. The coach can use this process to help client address problem behaviors and create new, empowering choices that are contextually appropriate and that truly fit for them and for others that may be affected.

Why do it?

The process helps the client to find creative solutions to problem behaviors and that can be implemented with minimal inner or systemic resistance. This process respects the fact that just about every problem behavior has a positive function supporting it, and it utilizes this idea to change the behavior while preserving the positive function. For example, smoking cigarettes might help a person to relax. Quitting smoking is difficult because the person will lose a habitual way of relaxing. To effect the change, the person needs to find another way to relax that is just as immediate and as effective.

How to do it:

1. Identify the behavior to be changed. Reframing works best on a behavior that you do but don't want to do (being late, procrastinat-

ing about starting to do certain tasks, not completing projects or activities, and so on). Name the behavior.

    a.   Explore the behavior to change and when and where it occurs. Get a clear sense of the "present state."

2. Separate the behavior from the positive intention. Find the meta-outcome of the problem behavior by asking, "What does doing that behavior or avoiding that activity get for you?" Ask this question several times until the benefit, the positive intention of the behavior, is identified.

3. Get agreement to try new choices. Ask, "If there were other actions that you could take, or other behaviors that you could do, that would work as well or better than what you are currently doing (to achieve the positive intention), would you be interested in discovering them?" (A "no" response indicates a misunderstanding, so restate the question.)

4. Create alternate behaviors to satisfy the intention.

    Help the client to access a creative state and brainstorm at least three new ways to satisfy the positive intention. Check to make certain that the new choices are as immediate, powerful, and effective as the prior choice in achieving the goal.

5. Bridging the Change into Action.

    Try out the new behaviors (in the imagination) in the appropriate future contexts to see how they might actually work.

    Ask the client or team if they are willing to take responsibility to actually do the new behaviors. Check to see if the client wants to be accountable, and if so, set up appropriate accountabilities.

6. Ask, "Are there any possible downsides, concerns, or problems that might occur as a result of making these changes?

    If "yes," modify the new behavior until the concern is fully satisfied. If no other concerns, then reinforce the new choices by rehearsing them mentally in desired future situations.

CREATIVE SOLUTION-FINDING PROCESS CASE STUDY

George's work unit was experiencing a common problem: most of the staff arrived late to the weekly staff meeting. After repeated and fruitless requests for everyone to be on time, George followed the steps above for a resolution. Most of the staff's positive intention was to avoid wasting time. If they arrived at the meeting at the last minute, then they felt they would not waste their time sitting around waiting for others to show up! Of course, the delay in getting the meeting going became longer and longer with this strategy, and the "solution" to the problem actually increased it and perpetuated it. The group brainstormed and quickly arrived at a solution that was not only simple but actually worked for them. The meeting time was changed to the first moments of the day each Tuesday. The staff, for the most part, made the meeting the first activity of the day and did not get involved in anything else first.

GETTING CLEAR ABOUT CRITERIA

Adapted from Dan Thomas, Focus Inc. Work is largely a process of decisions and commitments. Although the process was developed for the work situation, it can be applied in any life context. Many people feel conflicted or make poor decisions because they have not clarified their own criteria. The coach can help the client to determine what is truly important in a particular context, (work, marriage, parenting, friendship, project collaboration, etc.) or other situations, such as shopping for a car or house, etc.

Why use it?

To make better choices and decisions within an area of life

To increase the likelihood of finding fulfillment in life

To improve quality of life

What does it do?

Clarifies what is important in a life context

Identifies specific criteria that may be used for decisions

Ensures criteria are properly sorted and ranked

How do I do it?

NOTE ABOUT THE WORDS "CRITERIA" AND "VALUES"

We evaluate the world and make choices based on what is important to us. Values and criteria are words used to express what is important. Both of these terms reflect what is important and there is some overlap between them. Value words/phrases are more general and do not specify a behavior or condition. Values often go across contexts in life and can be applied in many situations. Values give direction and determine life satisfaction. For instance, you might value "freedom." But the meaning of freedom and how you determine this value is being met will likely differ in different contexts. Freedom in relationship to your spouse may be very different than freedom on a job.

Criteria words/phrases are usually more specific and are attached to a specific context. Criteria will provide a behavior or condition that you seek in a specific context. For instance, "flexible hours" may be a criterion for a job. Criteria provide a measure to determine whether a value is being met. "Flexible hours" may fulfill a value for "freedom" on the job. Criteria are used to help make decisions and to determine what is acceptable or unacceptable.

We title this exercise "getting clear about criteria" because we are asking the client to consider a specific context or a role. Then we ask the person to identify what is important within that context or role. According to the above definitions, we are asking for criteria.

Note: See pg. 30 for how criteria relate to Meta-Programs.

GETTING CLEAR ABOUT CRITERIA EXERCISE

Step 1: Identify the Context

The context can be any part of one's life that needs clarification or improvement. This might be career, relationship, lifestyle, health, etc.

Step 2: Elicit the Criteria

Ask, "What's most important to you about _____?" (your career, your relationship, your work role, etc.)

Write person's answer in big letters on an 8 X 11" sheet of paper. (It is important to use the person's exact words.)

Once you get the first answer, keep asking, "What else is important to you about _____?"

Keep asking until they run out of answers. A typical range is six to 12. Most people run out of criteria at a dozen.

Step 3: Rank the Criteria

Put the pieces of paper on the floor in the exact order in which the person identified them. Then ask them to arrange the pieces of paper from most important to least important:

"Please arrange your criteria starting with the most important first, and the least important last."

Then it is very important to check the order. Starting at the top of the list, have them stand beside the piece of paper and ask,

"Is the most important thing about (This context) criteria #1 ?" (Actually name the criterion they have stated.)

If you get a "NO" then ask what is most important and rearrange the pieces of paper.

If you get a "YES" then move them to stand beside #2.

Then, once they are beside #2, the language becomes very important. Preface this checking process by saying something like, "I know that what I am going to ask you next may sound unrealistic, but do your best to answer it and it will help you to rank your criteria."

"If you couldn't have #2, but could have #1, would that be okay with you?" Force it as an absolute - they have to choose one or the other. This forcing process will indicate which is really more important.

Observing the client's non-verbal communications will tell you the answer long before the client verbalizes it. If the answer is "yes," move on down the list. If the answer is "no," switch the pieces of paper and ask the question again. NOTE—If they cannot congruently answer the question, then there is some additional value. (It may be one in the list, but often is something that they didn't consciously articulate yet.)

Once the ranking is clarified, move on to the other criteria:

"Assuming you have the criteria already chosen (i.e. #1), if you couldn't have #3, but could have #2, would that be okay?"

Repeat this process until the list is rank ordered.

Step 4: Check for Missing Criteria

Once you have gotten the person's list in rank order, do a check for logic. You may find criteria missing. For example, if we are doing, "What is important to you about your business?" And "making money," "getting wealthy" or something related is not there, then there is likely a missing criterion. Say something like, "This is a terrific list of criteria. However, I am curious about something. This list is about your business and yet I don't see anything here about making money."

Step 5: Moving Criteria Up and/or Installing New Criteria

Once the "Present State" has been elicited, we know "what is." It will often be the case that it is obvious to the client that the ranking is not serving him/her well and that it is actually the source of some difficulty.

Ask, "Is there anything you would like to change about this list of criteria?"

The client may want to change the ranking, and/or install a new value if they have discovered one that is missing.

Experience indicates that: (1) typically, only the top three or four criteria provide substantial motivation toward action, and (2) the client and the coach need to have a VERY good reason to change a person's #1 value. Changing #1 will change a person's life. As always, be careful about the potential negative impacts of change.

Step 6: Cementing the New Hierarchy

Once the new or reshuffled value is in the desired hierarchy, have the client associate into (step into) his/her highest value and anchor them there. Then have them step backward, using appropriate language, such as, "And your highest criterion of _____ will be supported by your criterion of _____. "

Coach has the client walk all the way down the hierarchy. Then have them step outside of the criteria set to the side in order to check for congruency, ecology, appropriateness, etc.

Finally, start them at the lowest criterion and walk them UP the hierarchy, taking each lower criterion with them to support the next higher one. It is important to end with them fully associated to their highest criterion with all the supporting criteria.

GETTING CLEAR ABOUT CRITERIA
CASE EXAMPLE

Marjorie described ongoing tension between her young adult son, Brian, and her husband, Tom, which caused her and her daughter a great deal of strain. She emphasized that she really wanted them to resolve their differences, come together and restore family harmony. The holiday season was approaching, and she dreaded the thought of conflict during this time of year.

We used the criteria process to explore what is important to her with family. She listed a variety of criteria, including harmony, togetherness, sharing, supporting each other, etc. She completed her list writing each one on a card and laying them out in an initial order on the floor. The value of harmony came out on top when she went through the process of ranking them.

Marjorie realized that this value was so important to her that she had difficulty seeing beyond it. She felt excessive strain because she was "over-emphasizing" this one criterion and neglecting others. This insight alone began to put things in perspective for her.

I asked her to step back to consider if any important criterion was missing. I knew Marjorie to be a gentle person who valued love, but she did not include love on her list and I pointed this out to her. She was immediately clear that it not only had a place but was the top criteria. After adding this to the set and resorting them, she felt a tremendous feeling of relief about her family members. She again noted that she had been too focused on family harmony and now realized that she had neglected the overarching criteria of love.

With this insight, she was able to drop some of her anxiety about disharmony in the family and recognize the love that existed despite the differences. She realized that she had been "nagging" both her husband and Brian to resolve the problem between them. Marjorie later reported that she spoke with both of them and told them that she would love them both no matter what their differences. Within a few weeks, the atmosphere in the family lightened up quite a bit. Brian noted her change and confessed her that he had actually stayed away because he felt as much pressure from her as from the difficulty with his father.

DISNEY STRATEGY
(ORIGINALLY DEVELOPED BY ROBERT DILTS)

The Disney Strategy is a pattern for generating creativity modeled from the works of Walt Disney by Robert Dilts, one of the co-founders of NLP. The strategy is based on the ability to enter three separate states: The Dreamer, The Realist, and The Critic. Each state will have a distinct physiology or posture, patterns of thought, and feelings.

Why use it?

- To learn and use a very creative strategy for success
- To create clear goals or to turn dreams into reality
- To plan clear steps to achieving goals
- To ensure that goals meet specified criteria
- To evaluate one's plan to make certain it is what is really wanted and the downsides have been considered

What does it do?

Provides a clear strategy for goal setting and planning

Clearly distinguishes the functions for effective creativity

Provides a method for evaluating and refining goals

How do I do it?

Role	Mindset	Activities
Dreamer	This is the state of mind in which you dream of possibilities.	The Dreamer is concerned with what "could be" or what you "could do" and not with what you "should do" or "must do" or even "will do." For most people, the Dreamer involves creating visual images (visual construct eye accessing) and it often includes a feeling of excitement about new possibilities.
Realist	This is the state for creating plans and identifying steps to accomplishing a goal.	The Realist is concerned with how to make something work and not whether it will work or whether it is worth doing. The Realist identifies steps to accomplish the dream.
Critic	This is the state for evaluating the plan in relation to the outcome.	The critic's role is to find flaws in the plan, or missing pieces, and to determine if the plan really gets to the goal or meets the goal criteria. The Critic does not identify remedies. Disney stated that it was important to "get enough distance" from the plan to really think critically about it. This also helps to avoid criticizing yourself or other people.

- Identify a goal or desired outcome

- Become the dreamer - your goal is only to generate possibilities in relation to the goal.

- Take one of the possibilities and adopt a realist mentality. (Like a time when you planned something out). Your goal is to identify the steps to realize the dream.

- Step back from the plan. Get enough distance to examine it critically. Be like a movie critic – parts of the movie are great and some do not work so well. Identify potential flaws in the plan, or missing pieces; determine whether the plan really gets to the goal and is in line with your criteria, personal values, etc.

■ Take the information generated by the critic and recycle through steps 2 through 4 until you are comfortable that you have enough of a plan to take action.

Step 1
· Identify the goal or desired state
· The disney strategy helps create a more robust and complete outcome.
  It can be used during or after the process of creating a well formed outcome.

Step 2
· The Dreamer Role
· Step into the Dreamer role and vividly imagine the goal with all its
  benefits and possiblities.
· The dreamer is the big-picture visionary concerned with what is possible.

Step 3
· The Realist Role
· Step into the Realist role and create plans and strategies to make
  the dream a reality.
· The realist is like an engineer concerned with how to make it happen.

Step 4
· The Critic Role
· Step back from the dream and plan and enter the role of the Critic, sorting for
  gaps in the plan or mismatches with the criteria the dream is supposed to fulfill.

Step 5
· If necessary, recyle back to step 2
· Use information from the Critic role to cycle back through to steps 2-5, repeating
  these steps until the critic is satisfied or there is enough of a plan to proceed.

DISNEY STRATEGY CASE EXAMPLE

Denise was charged with producing the annual company party, a special occasion during this particular year because the company founder was also retiring. The management team wanted the retirement celebration to be a surprise. They gave her a budget amount, some general guidelines, and asked her to come up with a basic plan for consideration by the team. Denise brought this matter to the coaching session and we used the Disney Strategy to help her develop a response.

With the party goal in mind, Denise stepped into the dreamer position. She generated several options for location and party themes. The idea that appealed to her most was a Hawaiian/golf theme since the founder loved to golf and enjoyed Hawaii. She dreamed that the party could actually be in Hawaii, but she knew this was not within the budget. However, what she did imagine was a lively event filled with fun activities. She saw a "sand beach" with lawn chairs as the platform/stage where the founder would be toasted and his work celebrated. She saw a room decorated with Hawaiian images and a luau style party with Hawaiian delicacies.

She took this option to the realist position. Here she began to consider what was required to make such a party happen. She listed several specific steps, including:

*Research hotel sites or conference locations that could accommodate 300 staff and other "retirement surprise" visitors and be within budget

*Research catering of a luau style party

*Recruit help in decorating the site for the Hawaii theme

*Find the decorations and stay within budget

*Decide and coordinate party activities

*Establish ways to inform everyone about the "retirement surprise" while keeping it a secret.

She took this plan to the critic, stepping back from the idea to evaluate it, determine if the plan was complete enough to proceed, and whether or not it really met the criteria for the dream. From this position, she immediately realized the plan over-emphasized the retirement and did not take into account the annual party need. Plus, the plan was missing references to golfing.

She took this concern back to the dreamer to generate options to combine the two needs. She revisited her original vision and considered several options: one was to start the party with the annual events and then bring in the surprise after a period. She imagined a screen or curtain, which would open to reveal the golf/Hawaii platform. The platform would include some sand beach with a golf hole/flag, golf bags and lawn chairs.

Cycling this back through the realist, she identified the steps necessary to make this modification happen, including getting the sand, chairs, golf accessories, etc, which she knew would all be available from employees or family members.

The critic wanted to fill in additional information about the actual activities especially related to the retirement portion. She took this to the dreamer and imagined a "This is Your life" type game, where people from his past would talk about his life. He would have to guess who they were based on a few clues before they came out. The realist identified specific people from his past and present that might participate and how they could set it up.

The final adjustment offered by the critic was how to present this to the management team. Taking this through the three positions, she decided to create a "storyboard" of the party in honor of Walt Disney. The idea and plan was a hit with the management team who offered full support and even extended the budget slightly based on her additional research regarding costs.

BELIEFS

(THIS SECTION IS INFLUENCED BY THE WORK OF NLP DEVELOPER ROBERT DILTS)

What is a belief?

A belief is the acceptance of something as true or thinking that something could be true. Beliefs are essentially judgments and evaluations about ourselves, about others, and about the world around us. All of us have empowering beliefs as well as limiting beliefs. Most of our influential beliefs are outside of conscious awareness and have a huge impact on our daily thoughts, actions and general life experience.

We create our experience of life through our beliefs. The beliefs that we hold can shift as we learn new things and encounter new experiences, but often we hold them in a steady way and don't change them. Beliefs give us permission about what we can do and what to consider.

As Jan Elfline, Master Certified Coach states: As you work with clients, the first step is to make them aware that they have beliefs. This

BELIEF

NOUN:

1. The mental act, condition, or habit of placing trust or confidence in another: My belief in you is as strong as ever.

2. Mental acceptance of and conviction in the truth, actuality, or validity of something: His explanation of what happened defies belief.

3. Something believed or accepted as true, especially a particular tenet or a body of tenets accepted by a group of persons.

ETYMOLOGY:

Middle English bileve, alteration (influenced by bileven, to believe), of Old English gelafa.

SYNONYMS:

Belief, credence, credit, faith. These nouns denote mental acceptance of the truth, actuality, or validity of something: a statement unworthy of belief; an idea steadily gaining credence; testimony meriting credit; has no faith in a liar's assertions. *Definition from the American Heritage Dictionary® on line at Yahoo.com reference page.*

may sound absurd, but our beliefs are often invisible to us. We don't recognize our assumptions as beliefs. Instead, we think and feel they are simply descriptions of the way the world works. They go unquestioned and unexamined. In fact, we easily confuse our beliefs with "reality." Beliefs may be based on some evidence and may reflect some aspect of "reality," but they are still just a map or a model of reality. We tend to follow only the path our beliefs allow and neglect the fact that the world is richer and more varied than our beliefs permit us to see.

As your clients become sensitive to how much of their thinking is driven by the beliefs they hold, they will choose to form beliefs that will serve them. This may lead to a discussion about how beliefs are changed.

In *Beliefs: Pathways to Health and Well-Being*, we tell the story of a man who believes he is a corpse. On several visits, his psychiatrist attempts to convince him that he is in fact alive, but to no avail. Finally, the psychiatrist asks, "Do corpses bleed?". The man replies that of course corpses do not bleed, all of the systems in the body have stopped. The psychiatrist proposes an experiment to prick the man's finger with a needle to see if he will bleed. The patient agrees and when the finger starts to bleed, the patient looks astounded and says, "I'll be damned, corpses do bleed!"

This story illustrates a point about beliefs and evidence. Beliefs are rarely changed by our experience of contradictory evidence. People generally choose to consider only the evidence that supports beliefs or, as the story illustrates, actively distort evidence to support beliefs. If someone has low self-esteem, no external acknowledgment will make him or her feel worthy. If someone thinks of him/herself as incompetent, no number of degrees and credentials will convince them that they are capable.

As a coach, you can work at the levels of behavior and capability, and there can be great value for the client in making changes at those levels. But at times even after desired behavioral changes have stabilized, the client does not experience the benefits they expected as a result of those changed behaviors. The behavior has changed, but old beliefs are still running the show.

In contrast, when beliefs begin to transform, desired and lasting behavioral changes come about with less effort. As an old belief shifts, changing what we do seems natural and even inevitable. The old behaviors produce a feeling of incongruence. The new actions reflect current beliefs and "feel right."

In coaching you will have opportunities to address both beliefs about capabilities and beliefs about identity. From about the age of five onward, we develop skills and capabilities consciously by choosing what we learn. As we continue to grow, our beliefs about our capabilities expand. Children rarely question whether or not they are capable of doing something. They just try it. If they fail, they try again or in a different way. But as we grow older, we may try something several times, but when frustration sets in, we often assume that we are not capable and we never try again. As a coach, you may want to question the old evidence the client is referencing; how did they come to this belief about their capability?

As adults, we have little tolerance for moving through learning curves and we get easily frustrated and jump to conclusions about our capabilities. Albert Bandura at Stanford University studied how learning takes place and created the now famous Bandura Curve. He found that learning is a process of moving through crisis points. To progress, we must believe we can change or improve. As we believe in our capabilities, our performance rises to meet the belief. As we question our ability, our performance falters.

In working with clients, it is useful to assume that learning and change are processes that are influenced by our underlying beliefs. As coaches, we often speak about the processes of learning and change. We identify a dip as what it is, a stumble, not evidence that the client should quit striving for what they want.

Beliefs about identity often show up in the coaching relationship as "I am" statements. The client just assumes that "this is the way I am." Here again, the coach can challenge the client by suggesting that their statement is a belief. The coach could suggest that the client "try on" a different self-belief and notice what behaviors would follow from the new belief.

People often have a sense that change at the identity level is difficult or even impossible. In reality, we are constantly in the process of inventing ourselves. By deciding to work with a coach, the client has chosen to be conscious about the process of defining what their life will be like. In essence, they are inventing a new identity for themselves. Your coaching questions can help them shape the new identity they want to live into.

Beliefs are central to an effective coaching relationship. You will achieve limited success with private individuals or in businesses if you do not invite your clients to look at their beliefs.

LIMITING BELIEFS

Beliefs can empower you or limit you. They can give you the courage to tackle what others say is impossible or make you feel something is impossible no matter what others say. Helping clients to identify limiting beliefs is one of the most valuable skills in coaching. Fortunately, limiting beliefs tend to fall into four categories:

1. **Beliefs about Cause** – These are beliefs about causal sources of events and experiences. Often these beliefs have the word "because" in them. Some examples of limiting beliefs about cause include:
   - I can't be successful because my parents weren't successful.
   - I don't deserve to have what I want because I am not smart enough.
   - Life is a struggle because I never get what I want.
   - We're not supposed to have money because we grew up poor.
   - Money causes pain.
   - Being successful will cause the family to split up.

2. **Beliefs about Meaning** – Beliefs can also be about meaning. As human beings we are always trying to find the meanings in things. For example, what does it mean that we are poor, or that we are rich—what exactly is the deeper meaning behind these things? The meanings that we put on these beliefs will guide our behavior, because they operate as filters for our belief systems. Some examples of limiting beliefs about meaning include:
   - You did not respond to my hello and that means you don't like me.
   - Money is the root of all evil.
   - Taking time off means you're a slacker.

- Feelings are unimportant at work.
- Being late means you don't care about your job.

3. Beliefs about Possibility – Beliefs can also be about possibility and what is possible, or not possible, for us. There are two kinds of beliefs about possibilities:

The outcome is perceived as possible: If it is possible, then the person has permission from their unconscious mind to go for it.

The outcome is perceived as impossible: If it is impossible, then the person will not even bother trying to get what they want. For example, if you believe that you can't get ahead because the economy is bad and you hold that belief firm in your mind, then you won't do what it takes to be successful. You will give up ahead of time, and not do anything to create what you want. Some examples of limiting beliefs about possibility include:

- I don't have the magic ingredient that is necessary to be successful.
- Money is hard to manage. (I can't manage money.)
- I don't know how to make money.
- Large sums of money are for other people. (It isn't possible for me to have money.)
- How to make money is a giant mystery.
- If I make money, I will mess it up and lose it all.
- I will never be rich.

4. Identity – Beliefs that involve identity are about our worthiness and deservedness to attain wealth and success. Some examples of these kinds of limiting beliefs include:

- I am not good enough to be successful.
- I don't deserve to have what I want.
- I am not smart enough to make money.
- I don't have the right to live.
- I am not worthy of success.
- Nobody likes me, I am a loser.

Limiting beliefs tend to generate specific kinds of feeling states. When you encounter one of the following three feelings, you can be sure you are on the trail of a limiting belief:

1. **HOPELESSNESS** - Belief that the desired goal is not achievable, regardless of your capabilities. There is no hope that you will get what you want, because it is not really possible.

2. **HELPLESSNESS** - Belief that the desired goal is possible, but you are not capable of achieving it. You are helpless, and incapable of getting what you want.

3. **WORTHLESSNESS** - Belief that you do not deserve the desired goal because of something about you or because you are a "bad" person. Worthlessness may also arise because of a belief that you did or didn't do something that makes you worthless or undeserving.

Story about The Power of Beliefs

Until May 6, 1954, it was assumed that to run a mile in less than four minutes was impossible. In the nine years prior to the day that Roger Bannister broke the four minute barrier, no one else had even approached the time. Bannister surpassed the four minute mile barrier because he knew it was possible and that he could do it. Within a few weeks after Bannister's accomplishment, John Lundy from Australia lowered the record by another second. In the next nine years nearly two hundred people ran a mile in less than four minutes! The world no longer believed it to be impossible.

WHAT IS A STEM BELIEF?

A stem belief is a powerful underlying belief that holds together a cluster of supporting beliefs. Metaphorically, changing a stem belief is incredibly powerful because when you do so all of the supporting beliefs fall off "the grapevine" of limiting beliefs. The reason why it can be challenging to change a belief is because most people only work with the individual "supporting belief" instead of the entire belief vine, or cluster of beliefs.

It can be difficult to permanently change a belief without getting to the core of the belief. This is why affirmations do not work sometimes. They typically do not address the stem belief, they only address one of the smaller, less charged beliefs.

Most stem beliefs are formed when we are small children. They often sound childlike in nature and can be simply stated. They can be difficult to find.

However, with the right questioning, they can also be easily identified. Usually a person will get emotional, or they will even cry when they become conscious of their stem belief for the first time.

Once they acknowledge the stem belief and get past the emotion of recognizing it, they can begin the process of healing and transforming it. The success rate for changing beliefs is incredibly high when you focus on identifying and changing the stem belief because the stem belief holds together the whole cluster of related beliefs.

The most common stem beliefs that we have come across in our travels are:

- You have to work hard to make money.
- I'm not good enough to have what I want.
- I don't deserve to have what I want.
- Others come before me
- I don't exist, I don't have the right to be here

Questions and statements that help the client to examine beliefs:

- "What must be true for you to say that?"
- "(Backtrack their statement) because..."
- "What does it mean that _____?" (Repeat their sentence.)
- "Why?" or "Why is that true for you?"
- "Tell me more about that." or "Say more about what you just said."
- "How is that a problem?" (If you are unclear about that.)
- "What does that mean about you?" (Identity belief)

BELIEF CHANGE PROCESS
(ADAPTED FROM A TECHNIQUE DEVELOPED BY JAN ELF-LINE)

A simple belief change exercise involves heightening the client's awareness of a belief and the cluster if thoughts, feelings, and actions that surround it. Completing the following belief examination chart can often clarify what is at stake in holding a belief and stimulates desire to update and change beliefs.

Belief	Other Beliefs	Results
Belief	If this is true, what else must be true?	If all this is true, What actions will I take or not take?

The following case study demonstrates how this process works:

BELIEF CHANGE PROCESS CASE STUDY

Angie had worked hard to attain a level of success in the high-tech industry. She managed a small group of engineers and computer design specialist on a variety of projects. Yet she was unhappy with her career path. She had seen less qualified and less talented men receive promotions over her and felt she had been actively thwarted in her career advances. This topic came up on several occasions during our coaching work and she seemed ready to address the beliefs and ideas that she held in regard to these experiences.

I challenged Angie to consider that at least some of her experience resulted from her beliefs. At first, she thought this idea absurd because she had so much evidence that she had hit a "glass ceiling." I asked her to tell me what conclusion she derived from these experiences and she said, "Women are second class." We used this statement as a basis for completing the belief examination chart. Her assignment was to do her best to thoroughly complete the boxes on the chart. See chart and outcome on the following pages:

Belief	Other Beliefs If this is true, what else must be true?	Results If all this is true, What actions will I take or not take?
Women are second class	Men are first class; they will get more money and prestige for the same or even less work Women will always be treated as less worthy Woman have to work harder to prove themselves	Lots of resentment and anger, especially toward my boss A sense of resignation and a feeling of being stuck--I have given up on pursuing promotions Occasional commiseration with a couple of women colleagues, which usually just depresses me
Women are second class	I have to work harder because I am a woman No matter how much I do, I won't get what I want I have to be tougher than a man because any waffling on decisions is seen as my emotions getting in the way Men will be given the credit for my accomplishments	Often driven to do my best to show that I can perform as well or better than a man Occasionally complain to management about being held back; once formally complained but it lead nowhere Feeling that I am underappreciated and unrecognized

As Angie completed the chart, she became increasingly aware that her belief was itself causing her a lot of stress. We discussed the hopelessness she had developed because she believed that career advances were impossible for her as a woman. This provided an opportunity for coaching around this result. Our first step was to examine what this chart revealed that is important to her. Angie said it was most important that she be recognized and appreciated for her work. We discussed how she first needed to learn to toot her own horn in an appropriate way and at appropriate times.

I gave her the task of completing a list of her accomplishment on the job and how these had impacted the company. She started a running list over a two-week period completing several pages of accomplishments. In the process, she talked with some colleagues and co-workers who also gave her insight into her contributions and the impact they had on them and on the company. This exercise boosted her confidence considerable. Angie commented, "I was so caught up in feeling unappreciated that I neglected to appreciate what I had done myself."

Moreover, she felt less "edgy" when talking with her boss. Over the next few weeks, she began inserting references to her accomplishments at appropriate times in the conversation. She was shocked to hear her boss agree with her about one particular accomplishment. This made her realize that she had been silently waiting to be acknowledged rather than actively promoting herself.

Angie decided to take her whole list of accomplishments into the boss. Her approach was to give the list and say she felt like she could do so much more for the company and to ask him where she might apply her talents. Again, she was surprised when he revealed a couple of upcoming opportunities that might be suited for her. Angie reported that, in the past, she would have only heard about these kinds of opportunities after someone else, a man of course, would be given them.

As we reviewed what had happened, Angie said she still knew that there was definite discrimination against women. But she realized that she had unwittingly colluded in the discrimination by operating on her belief about it in an unexamined way. She now felt much more comfortable with her own accomplishments regardless of how much the world noticed. She felt more confident promoting herself and she believed it was more likely that she would find new opportunities either within her current company or by looking elsewhere.

IMPORTANT COACH REFLECTIONS

One of the seven habits of highly effective people, according to the classic work of Stephen Covey, is to "sharpen the saw." He uses the old metaphor of loggers competing in a log cutting contest. One works without taking a break and jumps out to an early lead over the second who stops periodically to sharpen his saw. Over time, however, the one who works without stopping must work harder because the blade dulls and cuts inefficiently. The second, who keeps the blade sharp, expends less energy and eventually overtakes the first winning the contest. Successful people take the time to step back, review their own skills, and work to improve them. This process helps the coach to "sharpen the saw." This process is very important for the coach, who can use the reflection to help keep roles clearly defined.

Why use this process?

- To sharpen your skills as a coach
- To coach yourself

What does it do?

- Encourages taking time to periodically reflect on your coaching process
- Provides questions for reflection about how you conduct your coaching
- Reminds you about specific principles of excellent coaching

How do I do it?

This reflection process guides you through a series of questions that you can ask yourself for continuous improvement of your coaching skills. Take some time every month or two to answer these questions. Be specific in your answers. Use your actual experience and answer fresh each time. It is best to use this tool immediately after a coaching session or set of sessions.

1. How do you know when you are doing a good job as a coach? What is your evidence?
2. How do you know when your client feels really listened to?
3. What is your sensory-based evidence that you are listening to your client?
4. How do you know when you are making a positive difference with your client? What is your evidence for this?
5. How do you hold back from giving information or offering a solution that you think would be helpful to your client (because you

know that the best solution will be the one that you draw out from your client)?

6. How do you manage and maintain your state as a coach?

7. How do you use powerful questions with your client? What coaching crafts do you use? How do you use them?

8. What is your "growing edge" as a coach?

After a few reflections, look over your answers and see if you notice patterns. Do you have challenges holding back advice? Are you using only a select set of coaching crafts? What throws you off track in your coaching, and how to do you get back on track? Coaching is a way to help your clients live more consciously and deliberately. We should expect no less of ourselves as coaches!

Putting It All Together

Coaching is one of the fastest growing professions because it is an effective resource for people who are serious about achieving their goals. As the many case studies and stories shared by coaching experts in this book have shown, the results can be absolutely transformational and life-changing. There aren't many professions in which you can make such a difference in the lives of others. Obtaining a strong, working understanding of the concepts and techniques we have taught here can make the difference between being an average coach and an outstanding one.

With such great potential to changes lives, and quite literally the world, we hope you will be inspired and motivated by what you have read in this book and will take additional time to further study and apply the Coaching Tools we have detailed as it takes time and practice to perfect each of these techniques. The work of coaching is largely a process of setting and accomplishing goals through individual and cooperative effort. Coaching draws out the strengths within people and allows them to grow and develop themselves, tap inner wisdom and motivation, and keep on track towards realizing their dreams.

It is important to always help your client keep sight of the role they play in their own transformation. You are there to guide, mentor and coach a person to discover the hidden resources they already possess. In the process, you witness them stretching beyond old limits, reaching out for the greatest potential they can reach, arriving at new horizons, and creating the life of their dreams from the inside out.

Coaching is a noble profession and we congratulate you for choosing to serve others in this way. We wish you the greatest skill and success in your endeavor!

APPENDIX I

META-PROGRAM PROFILE

(Adapted from the work of Rodger Bailey, used with permission)

Name: _____ Date: _____

Pattern	Question	Response
Criteria:	What do you want in a job? What is important to you in a job?	
Evidence:	How do you know when (criteria) is met? What indicates (criteria) is met?	
Direction:	What does having (criteria) met do for you?	Toward Away
Source:	How do you know that you have done a good job?	Internal External
Reason:	*Why* did you choose your current job?	Options Procedures
Mode of Comparison:	What is the relationship between your job this year and last year?	Sameness Progress Difference

Powerful Questions and Techniques for Coaches and Therapists

Pattern	Question	Response
Con-vincer channel:	How do you know when a co-worker is good at his or her job?	See Hear Read Do
Convinc-er Mode:	How many times do you need to (see, hear, read, do) this in order for you to be convinced?	Once Number of times Time period Every Time
Action Level:	Proactive people use active sentences Reactive people use passive sentences.	Proactive Reactive
Details vs. Big Picture	No specific question If we were going to work on a project together, what would you need to know?	Specific (small chunk) General (large chunk) Sequence
Attention direction	No specific question	Self Other Comparison
Time Ori-entation	No specific question	Past Present Future
Style	Tell me about an experience that was (<u>Criteria</u>) and what did you like about it?	Independent Proximity Co-operative

APPENDIX II

CASE EXAMPLES CONTRIBUTED BY ACTIVE COACHES THAT COMBINE COACH SKILLS WITH NLP THERAPEUTIC TECHNIQUES

Case Studies Submitted by Dan Ross

Dan Ross has combined 20 years of NLP experience with 25 years of working in industry in roles ranging from electrical engineer to COO. As a nationally recognized soft skills trainer, he teaches and coaches individuals and teams for measurably greater effectiveness in business and the workplace. He has spoken at national conventions and had articles on soft skills published in trade magazines. In his one-on-one coaching he is known for effecting deep transformational change in individuals, specializing in changing the unconscious beliefs that limit a person's full potential.

Dan can be reached at dan@svresults.com.

PERCEPTUAL POSITIONS:

Kathy felt like she was trapped. No matter what she did, she just couldn't communicate with her boss. After years of miscommunication, she felt like she was on thin ice. And it was causing her stress at work.

As we did our coaching intake, I could see that Kathy was smart, well-educated, and likable. I used the Meta Model to find out what specific situations were causing her problems. I taught her the three different perceptual positions and had her practice taking on positions as herself, her boss, and a third-party observer that could notice her behavior and coach her. Once she got used to that, I had her try on various work scenarios where communications with her boss had not gone well.

We started with e-mail communication. There seemed to be many miscommunications with her boss over e-mail. I had her imagine floating out of herself and into her boss as he wrote e-mails. I told her to imagine where he'd be sitting, his posture, and even his mental tone of voice as he wrote the e-mail. She could then connect with some of the non-verbal communication pieces that often gets lost over e-mail.

Next, I had her float into the position of a detached observer. I asked her to notice what an e-mail exchange would look like if she saw herself and her boss through the eyes of someone else. She could then visualize how things might play out in different scenarios depending on what type of reply she wrote. From this observer position, she could get a big-picture view of her communication style in general.

Using the same process, we tried out some other situations at work where communication had broken down with her boss. After that, she was able to better understand where her boss was coming from, and her communications over e-mail and in-person improved. Kathy reported back several months later that her career at the company had taken a step forward, and that she felt much less stressed at work.

THE META-MODEL

Back in the days when I was project manager, William, an engineer, approached me to tell me that the prototype we needed could not be built on schedule. As is a good idea when using the Meta-Model, I first "paced" him in order to maintain rapport. I did that by repeating his statement back to him with an inquisitive facial expression: "The prototype can't be built on schedule." Sometimes when people first learn the Meta-Model, they jump too quickly into using it to challenge people's statements. I wanted to focus on finding out specifically what was going on. Repeating his statement back to him diffused any concerns he might have about delivering bad news.

Then I started the Meta-Model questions with, "What prevents you from finishing the prototype on schedule?" He said a part that was needed was going to ship late. I asked a series of other questions to finish gathering information: "How specifically will being late prevent the prototype from being built? What would happen if you built it with a different part? How much of the prototype can be completed without that part?" All of these questions helped paint a picture of a viable situation. These answers also helped us to come up with an alternative. It turned out that we could use an alternative part that would have most of the functionality we needed, and would be good enough to make the prototype function properly and be delivered on time.

RESOURCE STATES

Joe never learned to read as a child. Now, at 75 years old, he was just learning to read. Reading by himself was okay, but he was terrified at the prospect of reading to a group, or even to his tutor. He had created a link in his mind that reading to another person equaled terror.

While interviewing him to find resource states he already had in similar situations, I found that Joe did not have a problem talking to a group as long as he did not have to read. I then guided him through the resource states process so that he would think of reading to people in the same way that he might comfortably speak extemporaneously to a group of people. I had him see the group differently in his mind; instead of viewing him critically, the audience was smiling and encouraging. I had him hear the group respond positively, even cheer him on. He learned to feel powerful and confident in his body while he imagined reading to a group. That created a new link in his mind that reading to a group could feel comfortable.

After that, I had him test his new resourceful state by first reading to me, and then test it again when he next met with his reading tutor. A few weeks later he was able to comfortably read a story he wrote to dozens of his fellow students and their families.

BELIEFS

Charlene never felt supported by the men in her life. Trust in relationships had been an ongoing issue throughout her life, and she was in a bad emotional state.

Having her focus on the thought of not being supported and the accompanying bad feeling that went with it, I guided her back in time to the origin of the limiting belief. This was traced back to when she was a baby. She was in her crib, crying out for her mother who was out to dinner with her father. Her uncle was baby-sitting, but she really wanted her mother. As a result, at that young age she adopted the belief that men could not support her and that she could not truly trust men. She had continued to operate throughout the years with that belief operating as a truism. As a consequence, she seemed to attract men who did not support her in her business and personal life.

Using the NLP re-imprinting process, I helped her find a resource state, then guided Charlene to see that incident with a fresh perspective so that she created a new belief about that incident in the crib.

When I checked in with her during a subsequent session, she reported that she was receiving support from men just fine, and wanted to know why I asked. Because beliefs form the basis for our reality, often when a belief is really transformed, the client can forget they ever had the old problem. That had happened to her. In the session, she said it had not really been an issue, when a month before she was very upset remembering all the times in her life when it had been a problem. Working on changing beliefs, rather than changing habits, makes it so that willpower is not required to keep the change in place. People just move through the world differently, and act with new behaviors automatically. That is what Charlene began to experience as an outcome of our work.

WELL-FORMED OUTCOMES AND GOALS

Whenever I work with a client, the first thing I do is ask them a series of questions to define what they want using a proven framework called the Well-Formed Outcome. Well-formed means the client's goal meets the following criteria: it is clearly defined, stated in the positive, any downsides have been considered; and that the person will feel happy once they have achieved their goal. This is a process that can be used with an individual, a team or a company. It can be as brief as a few questions during a conversation, or as involved as the framework for a multi-day corporate visioning meeting.

Below are a couple of questions that I ask all of my clients to help them get a well-formed outcome. I use these questions as a guide to help my clients set clear and achievable goals.

1. What do you want?

State your goal in the positive, and be as specific as possible with it.

2. Is the goal under my control?

Make sure to set goals that are under your control. Not "I want my boss to be nicer to me." Instead, it could be "I want to respond with curiosity and compassion when my boss is short with me."

3. Ensure your goal is appropriately contextualized.

Where, when, how, and with whom do I want it? Define the overall context of the goal.

4. Describe the evidence that will emerge from the procedure.

What will I see, hear, and feel when I have achieved my goal?

Imagine stepping in and having what you want. This will either give you more information, or may bring up something to resolve. For example, someone who has never had a lot of money may not be able to envision what it would be like to be free of financial pressure and believe in a sense of abundance.

5. Explore potential downsides to getting a goal

Sometimes getting a goal can create a problem in some other area of life. If a client has tried a number of times to make a change and they still have not gotten the result, there may be potential downsides to explore, even if the client is not aware of them yet.

For example, if going for a promotion, you might have to travel more and spend more time away from your wife and family. How will it impact those relationships?

6. What will having your goal get you that is more important?

This is a useful question that will help a client to get what they really want out of a goal. Sometimes a person can pursue a goal like losing weight, but not recognize they just want to feel better about themselves until asked this question. This can help prevent "buyer's remorse" that can sometimes come after achieving a big goal – that momentary good feeling that doesn't last. When you get to the "goal behind the goal" it can provide a deeper reason for wanting it, and a more lasting positive effect.

Case Studies Submitted by Epiphany Shaw

Epiphany Shaw is a NLP Master Coach and Trainer, Language and Behavior Practitioner, Hypnotherapist, yoga teacher, mentor and healer, specializing in helping her clients heal from infidelity, traumas, and past experiences that prevent them from living the thriving and fulfilled life they desire. For over 20 years, she has provided sessions for individuals, couples, and groups in the San Francisco Bay area and beyond. Epiphany has developed a powerful and integrated approach in her work and teachings, an approach that blends the workings of the human mind, her knowledge in business, her training in energy and trauma release work, her intimate knowledge of anatomy and physiology, with her embodied sacred outlook, all of which contribute to a full body-mind-spirit experience for her clients. She offers her programs virtually, in her Oakland office, or at her retreat center in Sonoma County, California. Epiphany's website is www.epiphanyshaw.com and can reached at epiphany@epiphanyshaw.com.

RE-IMPRINTING AND PERCEPTUAL POSITIONS

I have a client whose fiancé cheated on her. She was scared and confused, not sure whether or not to marry him and concerned she may never get over this trauma. To address her challenge, I used the Perceptual Positions technique to help her look at the incident from all sides: her fiancé's position, her position and even that of the person who cheated with her fiancé. We observed the situation by setting up objects on the floor representing each person, allowing her to view the circumstances almost like a play.

We discussed the situation in the third person, so she could be more distant, saying things like "he said" and "she said" rather than "I said." Then we spoke about how each person had not been resourceful, including herself. One at a time, we listed the resources that would have been helpful for each person involved. Her fiancé was confused and scared about marrying her, so he needed freedom, courage and integrity. Healthy communication would also have been useful. The woman who cheated with him needed self esteem, confidence as well as integrity. Together, we determined that my client needed clarity, understanding, trust in her instincts, perspective, understanding and most of all, forgiveness.

Once each person's needs were identified, using her linguistics to describe them, my client then stepped into each person and "became them" in that context, and received the missing resources for them. She became her fiancé and realized that if he had those missing resources, he might not have cheated in the first place. She then took on the role of the woman he cheated with and received her missing resources. Afterwards, she stepped back into herself and received all the resources she needed.

At the completion of this exercise, we took a break state, which is to stop the brain pattern and take a short recess or rest in which she was able to reevaluate how she felt about the situation. My client admitted that it still bothered her, but she felt more empathy for everyone involved as well as increased confidence. She now could see more possibility in the situation.

Everything in life comes down to giving and receiving love. I've noticed in my work that more than 95% of the people I coach arrive at a place of forgiveness, knowing we are human and not always resourceful. This understanding gives a deeper access to love.

I ended up working with my client's fiancé as well and learned why he made that choice, which was an unconscious way of escaping what he feared would be a bad decision after growing up watching his mom and dad fight until they became divorced. He was scared of love and ran from the situation. He was acting out the pattern he learned from his dad cheating on his mom. Even though we know the decisions of others, especially parents, may have been wrong, it is very common for children to make the same choices. By going back into his history and learning where his lack of resources came from, he was more resourceful, and with these assets was able to permanently change, so he could approach marriage with more commitment. In the end, the adversity actually brought more intimacy and trust into the marriage as they overcame it together.

SWISH PATTERN AND STATE MANAGEMENT

Jill was a professional singer who came to me because she was frightened before her performances after having tripped and fallen walking on stage at a large concert. Because of the incident, every time she stepped on stage, she was shaking and moving about in fear, instead of confidence. This was affecting her singing.

I used State Management questions to access what kind of state she wanted to actually be in at the start of her concerts. Through these questions, Jill expressed that she wanted to feel confidence in her singing and be connected to the musicians, audience and the world around. She wanted to feel a sense of belonging and be able to relax. Through the questions we identified that there was "play" in her ideal space. This was the resource she was lacking as she recognized that play is what would allow her to have a sense of humor about it if she fell, making light and fun of the blunder instead of having it become mentally disabling. Jill could also see that accessing the perspective of a bigger picture, would make a difference.

After using the state management questions, I helped her with tracking and anchoring past performances where she felt successful and had positive experiences so that she could call them into her mind and bring about the feeling of that state, no matter what happened. Once these positive states were anchored into Jill's mind, I used a Swish Pattern technique. This is where I would help her intentionally trigger her fears so that she could practice managing her state. We discussed what negative experiences would feel or look like so that she went into that state, and could practice bringing herself back out of it with the resources she had developed for anchoring the ideal state. When she was fully anchored in the positive state, we'd break state, and then restart on the present state triggering the negative state and then returning again to the positive. This is the swish pattern. We went through this exercise many times, with a break state in between, retraining her brain so that when she is triggered into fear, her brain will be automatically trained to move directly into the state of confidence.

Case Examples from
Karna Sundby

Karna Sundby has worked as a business coach and facilitator since 2000, helping people clarify their desired goals and discover the root causes which prevent them from achieving these goals. Using her expertise as a Master NLP Practitioner, Karna helps clients change negative thought patterns, painful memories, emotions and beliefs so they can get the results they want in life. She has worked with clients - children to seniors - whose issues range from stress-management to life-threatening disease. With 20 years of involvement in the field of human transformation and a 22-year career in management at American Express, she has the ideal combination of coaching proficiency, business expertise and a passionate desire to help clients make measurable transformations in themselves and their ways of thinking. Her clients have described her as highly-skilled, strategic, insightful, non-judgmental, energetic, clear and compassionate. karna@inneraccess.org

META OUTCOME QUESTIONS

Frank was a doctor who came to my office because he had gotten a DUI and was in jeopardy of losing his family and the successful career he had worked so hard to attain. In our initial intake session, Frank talked about feeling divided. One part of him was a workaholic, driven to succeed while another part of him wanted to relate to people and have fun, but this side needed alcohol to open up. Frank recognized that this part could ultimately create chaos in his well-ordered life, but he just couldn't control it. After getting his 3rd DUI, he landed in an alcohol treatment center. Now he was trying to pick up the pieces of his life and understand the underlying causes of his behavior.

As I asked Frank questions about this internal conflict, I noticed that when I inquired about his career and success, he responded very animatedly with his Right hand and arm. When I asked questions about his family, social life and drinking, his Left hand made a couple small gestures but mostly lay still in his lap. I observed that if he began to use his Left hand more fully, his Right hand would sometimes cover his Left hand, seemingly to hold it down keeping it motionless.

I used the Meta Outcome questions to uncover what each part ultimately wanted for Frank, engaging first with the workaholic part which seemed to be on the Right side of Frank. I asked this part what it wanted for Frank.

It said that it wanted to accomplish a lot. I asked, *"What will accomplishing a lot do for you?"* It replied that it would allow him to provide for his family. I asked, *"How is providing for your family of value to you?"* It replied that it would give him companionship in life. I asked, "What is your goal in having companionship?" It replied that companionship would lead to being comfortable with people and having more confidence. I asked *"What will having more confidence allow you to be or do or have in life?"* It answered that more confidence would lead to more success in his career, which would lead to greater self-esteem, which would lead to a feeling of self-worth, which would ultimately lead to a sense of Fulfillment.

The part which wanted to relate to people and have fun seemed to be on the Left side of Frank and had a difficult time feeling emotions, was shy and sometimes uneasy around people in social settings. Using the Meta Outcome questions I learned that with alcohol, this part could feel recharged, more open and engaged. I asked, *"What will feeling recharged allow you to be or do or have?"* It answered that he could then have more fun and be more spontaneous, have new experiences and feel good. I asked, *"What will having new experiences and feeling good get for you?"* It said that would enable him to have more confidence. More Meta Outcome questions led to discovering that more confidence would enable him to have more meaningful relationships, which would ultimately enable him to feel Fulfillment.

We were able to resolve the conflict between these two contradictory parts of himself once both parts realized they had the same values and ultimately wanted the same thing – to experience Fulfillment. Then they were able to work together on creating Balance in his life.

We discovered that without this understanding, each of these sides would at times demand to "be in the driver's seat" and dictate his behavior. When driven by success, Frank worked long hours, had little time for his family and felt isolated. To be comfortable in a social setting, have fun and feel more emotions, the free-spirited part would sometimes also go to extremes, drinking alcohol and creating chaos.

In the course of identifying the patterns motivating each part and the shared criteria of each side of his personality, I was able to help Frank integrate both parts of himself. He was no longer overwhelmed by his situation and began to develop a plan to create a balanced lifestyle.

I helped Frank visualize himself in the future having already achieved this balance and then had him step into his future self so that he could see through the eyes of a balanced Frank, hear through the ears of himself in balance, think the thoughts he would have when balanced and anticipate the feelings of himself in balance so that he could fully experience the state of balance in every part of himself. Then we created an anchor to reactivate this state whenever necessary to help him reorient whenever he felt that he was getting out of balance.

At the end of the session, Frank felt confident that he had the tools he needed to make the changes he wanted in his lifestyle. He recognized that there was more work to be done, but he could end the continuous inner conflict between his sides for the rest of his life because he understood the underlying issues.

We worked together to prepare for the State Board hearings and eventually they decided to reinstate his license. To date, Frank has put the pieces of his life back together and is a source of inspiration to others who have had problems with alcohol.

GETTING CLEAR ABOUT CRITERIA, AND MORE

One day a friend called and asked me to meet with her 15-year old daughter, Rebecca, who was having a difficult time adjusting to her new high school after having moved across the country.

When I met with Rebecca, I mirrored her body language, matched her breathing, used language which matched hers and quickly gained rapport. Feeling safe to be honest, Rebecca began to talk about how depressed she felt in her new environment. She told me that she yearned to have friends, date and be as popular as she had been in her previous school. As she talked, I could see how needy she must appear to fellow classmates. Rebecca told me how surprised she was when the "most popular boy at school" suddenly wanted to come over to her house to study. But once in her bedroom, with open school books, he began to pressure her sexually. Rebecca told me that she wanted to feel loved and accepted so much that she would have yielded to his requests. She confessed that the only reason she didn't submit to him was because of her own inexperience in the sexual realm and the fact that her parents were home and she was afraid they would get caught.

We talked about her conflicted feelings and I realized that Rebecca had no clear criteria about what needed to be in place for her to consent to experiencing intimacy. We began to chat about her values in life and then discussed more specifically how her values could guide her into clarity about what conditions would need to be met for her to become sexually engaged with a partner.

Rebecca left my office with a homework assignment to come up with a list of her criteria for intimacy. When she came back the next day with a surprisingly detailed list, I used the Getting Clear about Criteria process to rank the criteria. In completing the challenging task of ranking her criteria, she became even more clear about what was important to her and why.

Rebecca had listed things like:

- He will be a kind person.
- He will respect me.
- I will know him well before we are intimate.
- My parents will know and like him.

Using the some of the questions we use to create a well-formed outcome, I then guided her to clarity about what each item in her list meant to her. I helped her to develop truly well-formed criteria, rich with sensory evidence so that she would be certain when making this important decision in life.

For example, these are some of the questions I asked:

- He will be a kind person. *(How will you know that he is kind? Do you have control over him being kind? To whom specifically do you need to see that he is kind in order to know he is a kind person?)*
- He will respect me. *(How will you know if he respects you? What will he do? What will he say? How will you feel? Where in your body will you feel this?)*

- I will know him well before we are intimate. *(How will you know when you know him well? How long will you know him?)*

- My parents will know him and like him. *(How will you know your parents like him? Do you have any control over this? What is important about your parents liking him?)*

At the end of our session, I asked Rebecca to consider again "the most popular boy at school" and if he met her criteria of intimacy. She immediately shouted: "No way! I wouldn't even go to a movie with him!"

This process really changed Rebecca's whole perspective and she recognized her own clarity was necessary to be able to trust herself when making this important decision in life. She realized that for many of her peers, this decision is made impulsively, with no consideration of their own values, no thought about the consequences of their actions, not even knowing the person with whom they have just had sex and if they would ever even talk again!

I heard from Rebecca again when she was 19 years old. She called to tell me that she had just completed her first year of college and that she still had not gotten involved in a committed relationship.

She said half-jokingly, *"My parents say that maybe I need to lower my standards. What do you think?"*

I said, *"What do you think?"*

She said, *"I like my standards."*

I said, *"I do too."*

I saw Rebecca after her sophomore year of college and she told me that she had met a man and fallen in love. At first she couldn't imagine that someone like him, intelligent, handsome, fun, from a great family, en route to creating a successful career, would be attracted to her. But he was. They got to know each other slowly and when she felt that everything met her criteria – which apparently took a while! - They became intimate and are now engaged to be married.

A short while ago Rebecca's mother called to thank me for the work I had done with her daughter and said, "You changed her life." I knew it was true.

The next time that the "most popular boy in school" had found his way into her bedroom at a time when her parents were **not** at home, without any clarity about her own values and worth, Rebecca would quite possibly have found herself making a rash unconscious decision which could have changed her life drastically had she gotten an STD or become pregnant. And she would certainly have been left with the wounds of an injured self-worth after he had discarded her like a used paper plate, as he had done to many girls already. Her ability to trust herself would have been damaged, which would have affected future relationships. Her self-esteem would likely have been shattered and her innocence tarnished, never able to be reclaimed in the same way. There would likely be so much damage to "undo".

We all spend so much time and money trying to undo the consequences of what we have unconsciously created in our lives, whether that means trying to quit bad habits and addictions, free ourselves from emotional baggage born in the past, heal from the traumas we create by living unintentionally, change the limiting beliefs we developed about ourselves in our childhood, and the list goes on. It makes one wonder how life could unfold if we had the necessary guidance at each fork in the road.

It was such a fulfilling moment for me as a coach to listen to Rebecca's clarity as she said, "No way! I wouldn't even go to a movie with him!" And to realize that I **had** actually made a huge difference in the way her life would unfold. That was confirmed when I heard from Rebecca as a young adult and learned that the criteria she developed when she was 15 years old had actually guided some of her decisions in life. And then when her mother called to thank me for making that difference......wow!

What an incredible opportunity we have as coaches...to actually help people transform their lives!

BELIEFS

Robert had been employed by a large financial institution in their sales division for less than a year. He had moderate success selling accounts and was very well-liked by his team. After a year he had been given larger accounts to sell and his sales results declined. At the time of our first session, he was on a Performance Plan and had three months in which to improve his results.

His boss had accompanied him on sales calls and said that, in spite of his success with smaller accounts, Robert appeared to be nervous from the moment he stepped inside the office of a larger prospective client. When Robert **finished** giving his presentation, he would immediately relax and become his typical charming, charismatic self, asking the client questions about his family, hobbies, etc. Their sales force had specifically been trained to engage the client in personal conversations **before** presenting the product in order to gain rapport with the customer, but Robert was doing exactly the opposite.

As I worked with Robert to get to the root of his discomfort, he remembered an experience he had on the school grounds when he was about seven years old. There were two older boys who bullied him at the drinking fountain and then dragged him into the bushes and abused him. I asked Robert some of the questions listed on page 129 to help him examine what beliefs he may have formed as a result of this trauma. He quickly realized that he had formed this limiting belief: *It's not safe and I don't deserve to be here.*

We then used the belief examination chart below to further explore the effects of holding this belief he had formed when he was seven years old.

Belief Statement	Other beliefs: If this is true, what else must be true?	Results: If all this is true, What actions will I take or not take?
It's not safe	The world is dangerous. I can't trust anyone. I am powerless in some situations. More powerful people will hurt me. I am weak. I am a victim. I will never be safe being myself.	I must not let myself be seen. I must be invisible to people who could hurt me. I must stay small. I must be on guard. I can't relax. I can't be myself. I must figure out how to be someone who is safe. I must learn how to be someone that no one will hurt. I must learn how to be someone who will be liked and surrounded by friends so that I won't be hurt.

Belief Statement	Other beliefs: If this is true, what else must be true?	Results: If all this is true, What actions will I take or not take?
I don't deserve to be here	Powerful people deserve to be here but I'm not powerful and don't deserve to be here. I can't be myself around powerful people because I'm not good enough. I don't deserve to take the time and space of powerful people. I'm not comfortable taking the time of these powerful business people trying to sell them something that they don't want. I'm less worthy than the customers I'm trying to sell. The more uncomfortable I feel, the less product I will sell. I am a failure.	I want to take up as little time and space as possible. I rush through the presentation to get it over with so that I'm not taking their time. It's OK to be myself only after I'm not trying to sell them something. I've learned to be funny to be safe because no one hurts someone who is funny. I get rapport with people when I'm funny. It's the mask I hide behind in order to feel safe. When I'm done with the presentation I can put on my well-crafted mask and feel comfortable with the customer. When I try to influence him, I get nervous. As I get more nervous, I go through the presentation even faster and more awkwardly. As I get more nervous, I get less sales. As I worry about my results, I get more nervous and I get more and more scared that I may lose my job. I am hopeless and feel like giving up.

As Robert completed the chart, he became more aware that his belief was a self-defeating cycle which was not only limiting his success in his career, but could actually lead to the loss of his job.

In social situations Robert didn't feel that people were more powerful than he, so the belief wasn't as limiting in those circumstances. But he also became aware that he was never completely comfortable being himself. He wore the mask of the funny guy in order to be liked, fit in and therefore be safe.

I used a Belief Change Process developed by Tim and Kris Hallbom to help him transform his Limiting Belief into an Empowering Belief.

1. **Identify the Limiting Belief:** He used the chart to flush out the belief which was limiting him and how it had impacted his life.

2. **Find the Positive Purpose of the Limiting Belief:** I helped him identify how this belief had actually served him in the past. He described the violence of the neighborhood in which he had grown up. He realized that learning to spot and be invisible to the bullies had helped him avoid being hurt again. He also recognized that it was this incident which motivated him to find a way out of this neighborhood, unlike his siblings. He became the first and only person in his immediate family to go to college and thus land a job with a Fortune 500 company.

3. **Redefine the Limiting Belief:** Next we redefined the limiting belief by looking at it to see if it were always true and found that there were many situations in which he did feel safe and empowered. I also helped Robert see himself through the eyes of his mentor and peers to discover that they did not see him as weak or powerless. Quite the contrary. He was able to begin to see himself as others saw him - a resourceful, creative, capable, fun, caring problem-solver.

4. **Create a New Empowering Belief:** Redefining the belief helped Robert begin to consider a new belief. He ended up creating this New Empowering Belief: I have the power to be myself and get what I want.

Robert marveled at how a traumatic incident from his childhood had such a powerful impact upon his career. His sales results dramatically improved and he was removed from the Performance Plan before the three-month deadline. He called to thank me and we talked about how simple business coaching would not have gotten to the source of issue. Robert felt that something had transformed in his core and would affect his life personally and professionally moving forward.

Case Examples from
Austin Hill Shaw

Austin Hill Shaw is healer working in the medium of architecture, as well as a thought leader in the fields of creativity and innovation. He works with individuals who want to unlock their full creative potential and organizations that want to build cultures of innovation. He is the founder of 3 Lights Design, Creativity Matters, the author of The Shoreline of Wonder: On Being Creative, as well as the inventor of The Full Spectrum Client Intake and the The Core Needs Design Method, a ground breaking approach to architectural design that puts the core human needs—connection, making a difference, and meaning—at the heart of every project. Through his keynotes and trainings, workshops, retreats, online courses, and one-on-one coaching, his life purpose is to empower others as creators. Find out more about his innovative offerings at www.3lightsdesign.com and www. austinhillshaw.com.

A PRACTICAL APPLICATION OF NEUROLOGI-CAL LEVELS AND HOLDING THE CLIENT'S AGENDA

I do traditional coaching, creativity and innovation coaching, as well as architectural design. In all of these areas, I have found success with my clients by utilizing a technique called Neurological Levels. This is a way to get to know a person quickly based the various layers of a person's being, which include the physical body, behaviors, capabilities, beliefs and values, identity, and elements which are spiritual or transpersonal, all depending on their worldview.

To explain the Neurological Levels technique, I will give an example of how I have used it with my architectural design clients. In architecture and design, even when building simple projects, there are a million decisions to be made: What do you want a project to look like? Feel like? Appear on the inside versus outside? Will it be welcoming or private and secure?

When I meet a client for the first time, they have all sorts of preconceived notions based on what they've seen in magazines, family history, places they've lived, or things they think they want, and things they think they should have based on others' opinions. In order to access what is truly of value to them, and to turn their values into a design that actually reflects them as an individual, family, or organization, I use the process of Neurological Levels to establish the design criteria based on the following:

1. Environment
2. Actions
3. Capabilities
4. Beliefs and Values
5. Identities
6. Other

To be more specific, as opposed to having my clients sift through all the chaos in their minds about what the project should be, I take them through these different areas by asking the following questions:

1. **Where is this project taking place?** This may seem overly simple, but it allows them to ground into the space where this structure will be built… in the neighborhood, in the basement, in the backyard, etc. It roots their awareness into the physical space.

2. **What are the activities happening within the space?** Are you cooking? Cleaning? Doing laundry? Hosting parties? Raising kids? Holding meetings? Running a business? With this question, they are focusing on the activities that are actually happening in the space.

3. **How do you conduct these actions?** Playfully? Orderly? Religiously? Amidst chaos? Here my clients start to sense how their own way of doing things breathes life into those activities, which is the first budding expression of their belief and values.

4. **What are your beliefs and values?** Answers to this question may include: love, freedom, creativity, productivity, family, etc. It is important for my clients to give voice to these things. If I had asked this question at the beginning, it could be tricky to get more than canned answers out of them, but by moving through a natural hierarchy, beginning with the simplest question about where and what will be happening, my clients are able to incrementally look deeper and articulate these more existential questions.

5. **Who are you in this space?** Answers could be: I'm the uncondi-

tional loving host; I'm the super mom; I'm the handyman father, I'm the voracious bookworm, etc. In this stage of the Neurological Level process, my clients see who they are in the project and identify with it personally.

6. **What is helping you to do this?** This question extends the clients awareness to the webs of support that allow their lives and the project to unfold. A secular answer might be: the utility company, my neighborhood association, all those who have come through the house or built it; or they might say "God," or "Gaia," or "The Magic of the Bay Area." From this question, I get to the essence of client's worldview and help them to experience the project as something much more than just form and function.

Once we've gone through this series of questions, I turn the client around, and infuse the higher level criteria into the lower levels. For example, if something such as "unconditional love" is expressed as a value, I will anchor that value as an expression of an activity they mentioned early, as well in the future project. I might say, "See how helping you children with their homework is an expression of unconditional love?" In this way, the project is no longer driven solely by budgets, materials and aesthetics alone, but becomes a means for co-creation, self discovery, and self-expression.

Once the criteria is set, I can use them to facilitate decision making. For example, if they are stuck debating whether to add space to the kitchen or wanting an extra bedroom I might ask, "What would the unconditional, loving host do in this situation?"

By using the Neurological Levels, I can *Hold the Client's Agenda*, and design specifically around who they are as individuals or as a family. When going through the Neurological Levels, I work with husbands and wives separately as I don't want them to feel pressure to tailor their answers for their spouse. The conflict and paradox between their different values can lead to highly interesting design results.

While this example is a practical application of *Holding a Client's Agenda* while functioning in the position of a designer, this process also works effectively as a coach. In many ways, designing a structure is similar to coaching as you are helping your client to design their life to fit their beliefs, values, and goals.

GAINING RAPPORT

As a creativity consultant, I work to overcome the myth that some people are creative and others aren't. Creativity isn't a gift or talent of certain individuals, but is a defining trait of what it means to be human. Creativity is a natural expression of who we are, when we feel and trust our True Self. My basic definition of creativity is connecting with the world and affecting it in a meaningful way. You don't have to be artistic to be creative; being creative is a way of being in the world.

Working with coaching clients reveals that they have an idea of their identity; maybe it's negative, or overly ambitious, but they often don't have a true sense of who they really are, deep within, and what they are capable of creating. In order to get them to move forward, I must first experience their particular flavor of being stuck, which I do by gaining rapport.

To gain rapport with my clients and help them discover their true creative Selves, I take their posture, mirror their gestures, match their breathing and the pace or tone in which they are communicating. I use their same language, which allows me to 1) get into their world and 2) gain their trust. What establishing and gaining rapport by modeling their behavior accomplishes is to help people feel connected, and for me to better understand them from the inside out. In Western society, many of us are busy and overwhelmed. Interactions can be distracted or rushed. When you are able to mirror your clients in this way, however, they feel like you get them subconsciously and it helps them to relax into that state of self-existing creativity.

The joy for me is that I'm always learning from my clients. Though my role is the coach I often experience the client taking me on a journey. In the meta-picture, this is an opportunity to learn from the client and get past my own preconceived notions of who they are. I take their posture by sitting in the same way they are. If their eyes are going up in their head as they talk, they are visual and thinking and I tap into that eye movement. Others are very grounded in their seat, looking directly at you; I take note and do the same in return. Through this technique, I enter quickly and intimately into people's lives. It's both enjoyable and makes for effective coaching.

In some ways you might think that you would have to be subtle about this sort of mirroring, but the result is the clients sense compassion and empathy, and don't notice that you are intentionally imitating what they do. Instead, they feel physically "gotten," mentally "gotten," and maybe even spiritually "gotten" because you are focusing so much on them. Because of this effect on your clients –the power this technique gives you as a coach – makes it one of the most simple and useful skills to develop.

Case Studies from
Holly Stokes

Holly Stokes, The Brain Trainer, 3 time Author, Speaker and Master NLP Coach, has more than 20 years experience in the field of applied psychology. She has worked with thousands of clients in 'rewiring' the brain out of old habits, fears, stress and the sabotage that steals health and vitality. She created the A Lighter You! System to address the REAL reasons we gain weight and end yoyo dieting for good. Through Neuro-Linguistic Programming (NLP), Hypnosis and Coaching, she loves inspiring clients to lead healthier, happier lives of purpose and achievement. She has been quoted by Shape Magazine, Active Times and Chicago Tribune. She appears on radio shows and local TV in Salt Lake City, where she keeps a busy practice and co-owns The Life Harmony Wellness Center. She says, "Life, health, happiness, achievement - all gets easier with your brain onboard." Find her books and Hypnosis CDs online at www.TheBrainTrainerllc.com

RAPPORT

One day a client came in who was having difficulty at work communicating with his boss. He is graphic designer and his boss is in construction. As he described the situation, my client was distressed, repeating the phrase, "Why is my boss not getting it?" As he continued to detail the situation, at one point he explained, "My boss is so slow, it takes him five minutes to say something!" As he said this, my client was speaking very fast and I was able to quickly identify the problem.... He and his boss had differences in processing styles. The graphic designer (my client) is visually oriented and has a fast communication method. His boss is slow, and thinks carefully before speaking. During this coaching session, I spoke with my client about processing styles and differences in communication, helping him recognize that his boss wasn't failing to understand him, but that he had a different processing style which moved at a slower pace. I gave my client some cues to use when speaking with his boss, with the instruction to experiment with matching his bosses communication style. From this discussion, he became aware of the differences in their processing style, and relaxed more with that understanding, releasing the frustration. He learned that to talk with his boss effectively, he'd have to slow down. It didn't take him long to learn to match his bosses style; and he came back the next week saying things had really shifted in the relationship. He wasn't emotionally frustrated anymore and by slowing down to the pace of his boss, there was much less miscommunication. The boss was able to better remember what he told him and there was less friction in their relationship. By having the awareness of the different styles and using rapport skills, mirroring and matching the processing style of his boss with the same verbal speed – just that little change took away the awkwardness out of their communication and things became clearer and more positive between them.

RESOURCE STATE

One of my clients came in who was a new insurance agent that wanted to feel more comfortable and confident in talking to prospects about his insurance product. So I asked him how he feels going into a new building to make a presentation. He answered that he felt comfortable and confident in the parking lot, but as soon as he touched the door, it felt like his blood ran backwards, and he wanted to change this fear.

To address this need, I helped him create some positive resource states to draw from which supplied him with strength and confidence. I had him access positive feelings by thinking about happy memories. I guided him to recall a time when he felt especially confident and step back into that moment. While there, I had him attached some cues. The feeling had a color for him, which was red; so he anchored that state of confidence in the color red. In the course of this exercise, we set up another anchor to help him feel comfortable. This was the recollection of being at a family reunion. The color for that feeling was yellow. As he thought of those memories and the positive feelings associated with them, my client learned to think of the color attached to the memory and transport his senses. He created a visual image of the red or yellow color filling a bubble around him which suspended him in the positive feelings. It is from that resource state he could have his conversations and talk with prospects without the debilitating fear.

By using his color cues, my client could quickly draw from this resource state in circumstances when the fear crept in. Before he walked into a building or a meeting, he began mentally stepping into this state until the fear went away. Shifting away from focusing on the fear, he recognized how he was able to portray confidence in his product, so it boosted his sales result as well as helped his comfort.

Index

John Grinder iii, 4, 52

K

Karna Sundby iii, 147
Kris Hallbom ix, x, 14

L

Language 27, 28, 29, 30, 31, 32, 33, 34, 52, 53, 54, 56, 58, 60, 62, 75, 76, 79, 81, 97, 115, 116, 149, 159
Nick LeForce ix
Thomas Leonard iii, 3
Leslie Cameron Bandler iii, 22
Active Listening 41
Lost Performatives 54, 58

M

State Management 93, 146
Managing Client Sessions xi, 3, 6, 9, 71–97
Ian McDermott iii
Meta-Model 52–60, 64, 139
Meta-Outcomes 84–88
Meta-Programs iii, xi, 12, 22–35, 113, 136
Mind Reading 54, 59
Modal Operators 54, 57
Mode of Comparison 28, 136
Motivation 2, 6, 12, 22, 25, 26, 35, 67, 84, 86, 88, 116, 135

N

Neuro-linguistic programming (NLP) iii, ix, x, 4, 41, 52, 66, 72, 73, 74, 78, 83, 118, 123, 138, 139, 142, 144, 161
New Behavior Generator 105–107
Nick LeForce ix
Nominalizations 53, 55

O

Open Questions 50–52
Modal Operators 54, 57
Options People 27, 28, 34, 136

P

Made in the USA
Monee, IL
27 July 2023